Tucks and Textures

Two

by

Jennie Rayment

D1439659

Acknowledgements

This book is dedicated to Nick Diment without whose unfailing help, support, advice and encouragement, none of this would ever have happened. He has coped with tantrums, tears and distress, jollied me along and administered a good kick (metaphorically) when necessary. Marvellous man!

A very special thank you must be given to Basil Crisp who has waded through all my ill-written proofs, messy punctuation and howling grammatical whoppers, and still speaks to me! In addition, my thanks are extended to Derry Morgan, the printer, who, once again has come up trumps; and John Plimmer, the photographer, for his superb photography. Not to be forgotten, Vic Harley for all his hard labour and effort in laying out the pages.

Also, my thanks and gratitude to Pam Balls, Chris Day, Lynette Harris, Shelagh Jarvis and Val Morgan, who have kindly lend me their work for the photographs. A further thank you must be extended to all the students who have borne with fortitude my teaching, listened to my lectures, laughed and giggled with me, and who still come back for more. (One delightful lady even mopped up the tears at a Quilting Show on a never-to-be-forgotten day.)

Finally, thanks to my parents especially my mother, who has listened to the moans and groans, shared the highs and lows, and still keeps a kipper by the back door!

Copyright © Jennie Rayment 1997
First Published May 1997 by J.R. Publications
Wren Cottage,
3 The Millstream,
Haslemere, Surrey GU27 3QA.
Tel/Fax: 01428 652495 / 01243 371742

All rights reserved. No part of this publication may be reproduced, transmitted or stored in any form or by any means without written permission from Jennie Rayment.

ISBN 0-9524675-6-9

Photography by Japics
10 The Pallant,
Havant, Hampshire PO9 1BE
Tel: 01705 476624/470310

Printed by St. Richard's Press Limited
Leigh Road, Terminus Industrial Estate,
Chichester, West Sussex PO19 2TU
Tel: 01243 782988

Contents

International Distributors

Quilter's Resources Inc.
P.O. Box 148850, Chicago,
Illinois 60614, U.S.A.
Tel: 773 278 5695 Fax: 773 278 1348

Margaret Barrett Distributors Ltd.
19 Beasley Avenue,
P.O. Box 12-034, Penrose,
Auckland, New Zealand
Tel: 64-9-525 6142 Fax: 64-9-525 6382

Tucks and Textures

Two

You have seen the book - **'Tucks Textures & Pleats'**, got the T-shirt and searched for the video! Well, unlike 'Jaws 2' and other films and books of that genre, this is not a continuation of the first unmitigated success; but it is a totally new compilation of ideas and projects and can stand by itself.

Yet again you will be exhorted to play, create and experiment with the new techniques writ in this perambulation through the ways of fiddling with fabric.

We will discover the novelty of dyeing, no not dying - there is an 'e' - the latter is a little final and could hardly be described as novel. We investigate more ways to nip and tuck material and there are several projects for you to construct when you have a spare moment. There is even an investigation into the feasibility of using Fibonacci. Once again you will be persuaded to tumble into the depths of iniquity and sup a glass or two of alcoholic liquor, and together we will muddle through the fascinating maze of textural niceties and even do a bit of sewing as well.

Since the birth of the previous book, my life has become one mad journey after another, hurtling up and down some dreaded motorway in search of yet another Scout hut at the back of Acton or was it Manchester, Liverpool, Bognor or even Accrington Stanley? The M25 is a well trod line and I can achieve a fantastic quarter-inch seam allowance down the central lane! It has been said that an addiction to the sewing machine improves your driving skills. It is a pity that I am unable apply such skill to the computer; steering my way through a morass of files, data and further computing rubbish is much harder than dreaming up a new way to tuck a bit of material. Nowadays I travel internationally to teach 'Nipping and Tucking' as my family refer to it, which is a euphemism for plastic surgery in the States, and if you think for a moment - that is exactly what I do - give fabric a face lift!

So, my friends, enough of this nonsense, let's launch into another excursion with fabric manipulation and textural bits and bobs and in the infamous words of the last publication -

You can't go wrong,
it's just a little different!

About Tucks and Textures Two

It was decided not to repeat all the information from the beginning of the last book but for those who do not possess **'Tucks Textures & Pleats'** here is a selected precis.

Choice of Fabric

For many of the samples in **'Tucks and Textures Two'** I decided to use **Calico** (unbleached cotton material). **In the U.S.A. this particular cloth is referred to as MUSLIN,** but any kind of fabric may be selected for texturing although natural fibres are easier to manipulate. The reason for selecting this type of fabric is both for economy and personal choice. Calico is not expensive compared to other materials and students prefer to use a fairly cheap material when experimenting with all the different techniques; in addition I produce a vast amount of teaching pieces using yards of cloth which could get very costly. Also, the pale colour of the material reveals the pleats and folds of the manipulations very well. It would be difficult to actively dislike the material due to its neutral colour and composition; consequently one can give items made from calico to anybody. There are few places where this cloth will look out of place.

The type of calico that I normally use is an inexpensive medium-weight firmly woven material which can be purchased in many places from department stores to local street markets and dress making, interior design and quilt shops. It comes in a variety of widths and shades of cream often with an attractive dark fleck. Personally I like a slightly stiffer material to work with as it is easier to manipulate, rather than the lovely sheer calico/muslin used for backing quilts and/or hand-quilting. This latter type is a trifle fine for easy manipulation but it really does not matter too much. Some of the techniques will lend themselves to a thinner weight of fabric, others to a firmly woven heavier weight of cloth. Should you choose to make the designs in miniature, I would advise use of finely woven light-weight material.

Although I love the effect of calico, textural creations can look wonderful in all kinds of fabric from chintz (glazed cotton), satin, denim, sateen, thin suedes or leathers, cretonnes and silk. The glazing of chintz reflects the shadows of any texture very well and can sometimes resemble a smooth leather. If you select a fine silk try ironing on to the back one of the fusible interfacings to prevent fraying and add a little more 'body' to the fibres. Use of a spray starch will add extra support to thinner materials such as lawn (fine smooth cotton cloth with a crisp finish), which helps when manipulating the surface.

Explore the use of pre-textured cloth, patterned fabric and directional designs. Stripes really lend themselves to surface manipulation as you can play with the lines to add a further dimension to the design. Experiment with pre-textured material to enhance the desired creation. Patterned fabric can have an interesting effect but the pattern should not be too large or you will loose the definition of any texture. Colour plays an important part although the lighter the hue the more the texture will show. Black or very dark shades may obscure the intended impression but I have seen some fascinating pieces created from black chintz. As a beginner it is probably preferable to use pale tints to start with.

On the subject of laundering, I have to admit that I never pre-wash my fabrics before use. There are two reasons for this, firstly I am too lazy to iron out the creases; have you ever tried pressing over-dried calico? Secondly and more importantly the dressing in the cloth stiffens it. As you will appreciate anything that is a little stiffer is probably easier to manipulate, however I would advise washing the material if it is to be used for babies or toddlers and/or making garments in light coloured fabrics. As a general rule if you prefer to pre-wash then do so and try spray starch to add the extra 'body'; but if you like the lazier method then don't pre-wash. (In **'Tucks Textures & Pleats'** full instructions for washing finished items is given on page 12.)

****

'Tucks and Textures Two' is written in a light-hearted manner with plenty of diagrams and easy to follow instructions. The book begins with 'Vandalism' which is an extremely easy way to texture fabric and then follows a path through new ideas for surface manipulation and unusual textural effects. **The sequence of the chapters bears no relation to any degree of difficulty; they are simply laid out in an interesting manner**. There is also a section which contains some of the ideas from the previous book but in greater detail such as 'Tucked-up Circles'.

Tips or special points to watch are identified with bold-faced italics.

It is intended to be used a workshop manual working through the techniques in any one chapter stage by stage. You are not supposed to leap to the end and guess the middle bits!

For American use

Remember that British Calico is U.S.A. Muslin and the phrase 'catch it down' means to 'tack it down'.

In England we often refer to several small stitches in one spot (used to secure a corner or edge) as a 'catch', and 'tacking' is a series of long stitches (used to anchor layers together before sewing firmly). I had a salutary lesson when I visited the States as I asked the class to tack something and to my amazement they very carefully stitched it. (I wanted them to run a series of large stitches across the work similar to basting.)

Read on and enjoy the book.

<u>Vandalism</u>

Let us be destructive and ruin some perfectly good material. Too many husbands or maybe partners/friends say that they fail to understand how we can purchase lovely cloth, cut it up and then stitch it back together. This does appear to be somewhat strange behaviour but as we all know, it is in the interests of creativity. Now we will not only cut it up and stitch together but inflict wanton damage upon it. There is probably something fundamentally wrong with me (rude comments are not appreciated), but there are odd occasions when I enjoy destroying something. Do not fret though - this is a fairly intentional destruction and can have very creative effects.

I have always been a trifle scathing about slashed fabric until I discovered this technique and can now see the delight of hacking through layers of cloth. In the previous book **'Tucks Textures & Pleats'** there was a section referring to slashed material where you layered a selection of different materials, stitched a pattern of lines through the pad to form a square grid then cut through the layers (not the bottom one) on the bias before washing and tumble drying etc. This method needs no washing or tumble drying: the textural surface happens immediately as you will see.

The name for this technique arose when I was teaching a class in Suffolk and I overheard one lady whisper to another `I think we are into vandalism now'. Still, better this than other forms of deviation.

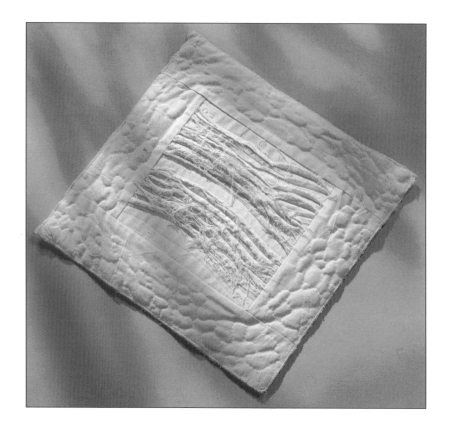

Creative Vandalism

The technique looks great in one colour but there is no reason why you cannot use a variety of coloured materials. Try it and see. Should you choose to experiment with silk, **do not back with a fusible interfacing as it will not fray so easily**.

1. Cut five squares or rectangles of material all the same size. Place one on top of the other R/S up; pin the layers together.

2. Select a slightly longer stitch on your machine than recommended for normal stitching (the thickness of the materials will contract the stitch length). Sew across the pad of material in an irregular manner (Fig. 1). This is not difficult!

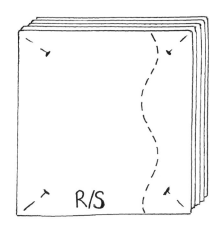

3. Repeat this stitching, keeping the lines of stitch approximately ½" (1.25cm) apart. (It will be difficult to cut between the rows if the stitching is too close together.) However, you can always sew the rows further apart. Keep going, changing the design as you wish (Fig. 2).

4. With sharp scissors cut between the rows, *cutting all the layers but the last one.* Disaster will strike if you do and *please do not attempt with the rotary cutter.*

5. This looks pretty boring but there is a secret weapon - **the iron!** Rub the iron firmly over the surface from side to side across the work. It will begin to fray and become raggedy. (Makes a splendid mess on the floor.) Stop ironing when you feel that the surface is frayed/tatty enough. Or distress the surface is by rubbing the R/S vigorously .

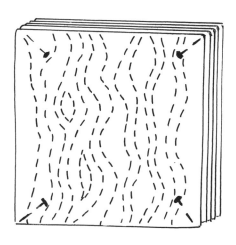

Figs. 1 & 2

Add borders and it could be a small textured wall hanging. Cut it into pieces and stick on to handmade cards. Embellish with some beads. Make several squares and stitch together, arranging in a pattern. For a 'wacky' garment insert strips into the bodice or sleeves. It is not the most robust of textured surfaces so launder it infrequently, and keep little fingers away as they may feel inclined to pull all the frayed edges out.

Great idea for embroiderers or those suffering City & Guild courses or other textile design studies.

Further Ideas for Vandalism

Design a panel developed from the lines in bark, crevices in rock, cracks in glazed china, in fact any set of lines running across a surface. How about starting in the centre and sewing outwards (Fig. 3)?

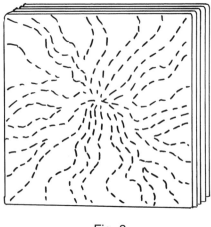

Fig. 3

Do you have to cut all the layers all the time? Try cutting some of the layers in one section and all of the layers in another area.

Experiment with colour. Explore the possibilities of different coloured layers and see what happens when they are frayed.

N.B. A small piece of sticky tape/sellotape will remove the mess on the carpet.

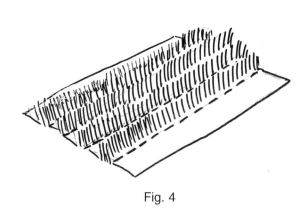

Fig. 4

An additional idea for an attractive effect with frayed surfaces came from a lady at West Dean College. She had made a panel of closely spaced thick tucks which were too difficult to flex in any way. Rather than waste the sample, she slit all the edges of the tucks then frayed them (Fig. 4). The result was similar to the spiky hairs on the back of caterpillars or the soft furry appearance of a very short hair-cut.

Interlocking

Textured Shapes

Technically an interlocking shape is a tessellation. The word derives from the Latin - tessera (plural tesserae), which is the name given to the small square pieces of stone used to construct mosaic pavements and murals back in ancient times. (This was even before I was born!) The square shape was used because it fits together to form a solid pattern without any gaps in between - extremely useful as Romans meandering over the pavements did not trip and break their necks. (Would the Fall of the Roman Empire have happened earlier if the pavements were not composed of snuggly fitting pieces?) Not all tessellations are squares and other geometrical shapes will tessellate i.e. hexagons and equilateral triangles; even rectangles will interlock.

There are various books written on constructing tessellations which describe how to make symmetrical and asymmetrical tessellated shapes. One day I may write a light-hearted tome on the fun things to do with tessellations and easy ways to make them.

Rest assured, here we have only simple ones, merely textured and interlocked sections created from overlapped and interwoven shapes. Wow! I expect that has put you off instantly and you will toss the book in the bin in disgust. It sounds really complicated but in reality is very simple.

Relax.

Turn the page over and see how easy it is. You will *not* need a large glass or two of an intoxicating stimulant to be able to do this.

Interlocking Squares

To create a panel 12½"(31cm) square, you need 16 x 6½"(16.5cm) squares cut from the fabric of your choice. Different colours or types of materials could be selected but try making one of the sections first from some scrap fabric *before* you make any big decisions: then you will see how the design fits together.

To make one section you require 4 x 6½"(16.5cm) squares. Cut all the squares from the same fabric for the first attempt. (The suggested size is not important; so any scraps that are square will suffice to make a sample.)

 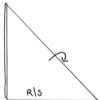 Fig. 5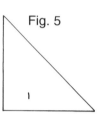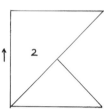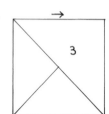

1. Fold squares on the diagonal, R/S out, and press - forming triangles. Lay the triangles down in the following manner (Fig. 5), rotating each successive triangle through 90° and *tucking the last triangle under the first*. Pin the layers carefully together. Using the longest stitch length possible on your machine sew closely round the outer edge.

Figs. 6 & 7

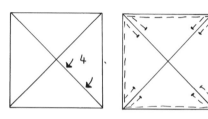

2. Carefully roll back the folded (bias) edges of the triangles **by the same amount**; pin down. Turn the block over to check that the fold is correct on the back. Magically a square hole will appear in the middle (Fig. 6). At this point you could stop as the patch is double sided with a textured roll one side and a fold on the other.

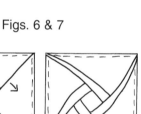

3. Place the block on to a scrap of material, centring the hole over the scrap. (This scrap could be a different colour or texture to the rest and a small piece of wadding/batting may be positioned beneath.) Using a tiny hand stitch secure the edges of the folds through all the layers (Fig. 7).

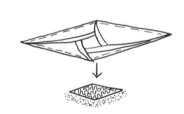

For an interesting design, try some free machine quilting on a spare piece of material and use this to fill the central hole. (Free machine quilting is mentioned in the last book and is memorable for its alcoholic content.)

For those who do not possess the last book here is a re-run of the text:-

Free Machine Quilting

There is no doubt that practice makes perfect; well, it improves it. This is one of those techniques that needs a relaxed operator (glass of wine recommended before commencing). Push the sewing machine further away than normal. Sit comfortably; lean towards the machine keeping the spine straight, pushing your bottom out and rest your elbows on the table to take the weight. The wrists need to be free and flexible. Relax and drop your shoulders; students with rigid shoulders up under their ears do not perform so well.

So you are sitting correctly, have consumed the vino and have relaxed. You have lowered the feed dogs, attached the darning foot, positioned the work under the needle and all you have to do is construct a series of rounded squiggles. These should not cross over each other nor have points or spikes, but flow evenly over the selected area as in Fig. 8. *Bet the telephone rings!*

Fig. 8

Try it; grasp the material firmly, do not have flat hands. Bring the lower thread to the top surface to prevent it tangling underneath. Maintain an even speed as you swing the work in a series of arcs (similar to steering a car). **Relax!**

Some sewing machines do not have a darning foot but there may be a lever or knob that controls the amount of pressure on the presser foot (see instruction book). By reducing the pressure to zero and using the ordinary presser foot, it is possible to free machine quilt although not so easily as with a darning foot.

Using this technique will enhance the textural effect. It is difficult at first but keep experimenting and if you can't achieve the random curves - have spikes!

Now you too can do it - free machine quilting that is.

Having made one square interlocking textured block, make a further three. *Watch that you lay them all down in the same fashion or the triangles will rotate in different directions.* Using a variety of coloured materials will enhance the effect and playing with clockwise and anti-clockwise rotations of the triangles will also change the total appearance.

Interlocking Equilateral Triangles

Equilateral triangles are so called as all the sides and all the angles are equal! The name comes from the Latin - *aequilateralis* (equilateral). My father insisted. that I studied the language at school as many words in English have their derivative roots in this classic tongue and you can see how useful it is! To this day I can still decline the noun `table' in all its forms, discuss knowledgeably the plural gerundive form of table, and my ability to quote from Caesar is a good dinner party conversation stopper - but I digress.

To construct an equilateral triangle you have a choice. There are various geometrical rulers sold in Craft and Quilt shops in a range of sizes or you can make a template.

To make a template decide on the length of the sides - *remember this length will not included seam allowances: these are added after the construction. You are drawing the finished or real size.* Rule a line this length in the middle of the bottom of the page. Let's call the ends A and B.

With a pair of compasses, place the point in A and stretch the pencil to B. Draw an arc above the line. Keeping the instrument at the same measurement, insert the point at B and draw another arc crossing the previous one; call this C. Join AC and BC and there is the equilateral triangle (Fig. 9).

Now add the seam allowances to all sides.

The same type of triangle can also be constructed with a protractor.

Rule the same AB line. Place the protractor on A (watch that the protractor is positioned accurately) and measure 60°; make a small dot. Put a ruler on A and passing through the dot, rule a line the length of AB. Repeat this at B using the other side of the measurements on the protractor. The two lines will meet at C (if you want to check the accuracy measure the angle at C - it should be 60°).

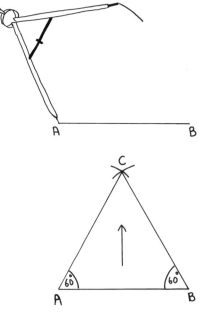

Fig. 9

Now add the seam allowances to all sides.

Make card template or use template plastic and trace off the shapes including the seam allowances. *Always indicate the straight grain line with an arrow.* (The grain line will run up the centre of the triangle.)

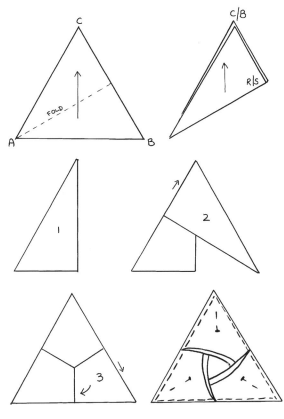

1. Cut out triangles in sets of three. Fold in half R/S out, and press. ***The fold has to be across the bias grain*** (Fig. 10). Failing to do so results in less easily manipulative folds.

2. Lay the triangles in the same rotating manner as in Fig. 5 before, tucking the last one underneath the first. Pin well and 'stay' stitch (use a long stitch length) on the outer edge. (Stay stitching is the same as tacking - English, basting - U.S.A.).

3. Roll back the edges of the triangles as before. There will be a triangular window in the centre. If desired place the shape on to another scrap of material to cover this space. Catch the edges of the folds down through all the layers (Fig. 11). See page 19 for more ideas.

Figs. 10 & 11

Interlocking Hexagons

A hexagon is probably the most common tessellation after a square. It is very easy to construct although one can purchase hexagonal shapes to draw round, but why bother when all that is required is a pair of compasses?

Decide on the size of the hexagon. The size is determined by the distance from A - B which is across the widest point (between the opposite corners). Set the compass for half this measurement and draw a circle. ***Do not move the compass setting.***

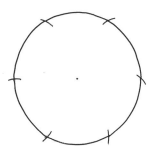

Place the compass point at any place on the circumference (circle edge) and draw an arc crossing the line. ***Replace the compass point exactly where this arc crosses the circumference*** and draw a further arc. Repeat until you come back to the beginning; the last arc should pass through the initial point of insertion. Should it not - do it again and try to be more accurate; ***do not move the compass setting.*** Rule lines from the all the intersections of the arcs and circumference (Fig. 12).

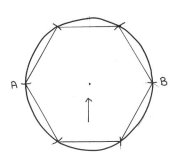

Fig. 12

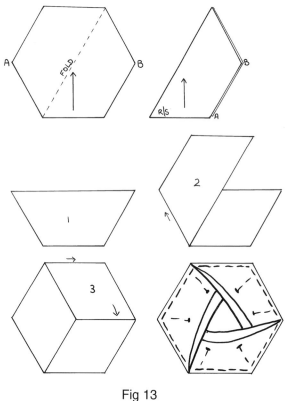

Fig 13

There are other ways to make hexagons but this is the simplest. *Add the seam allowances to all sides and insert the straight grain line.* Make a template. Cut out hexagons in multiples of either three or six. Fold in half - R/S out - across the bias grain and press.

a. Three hexagons can be interlocked by placing on alternate sides as you rotate them. *Tuck the third under the first* (Fig. 13). Pin well and stay stitch. Roll back the folds as before. There is still a triangular space in the centre; conceal the hole as described previously.

b. Six hexagons are interleaved as previously with one hexagon to each side (Fig. 14a). Repeat the pinning and stay stitching. Roll back the folds; now there is a hexagonal hole in the middle.

Place on a scrap of material and/or wadding and catch the centre folds down. As there are so many layers you could trim parts of the shapes away; ensure that there is still enough to roll back

c. Four hexagons can also be interleaved and magically a diamond shaped space will be revealed in the centre (Fig. 14b).

d. Explore the effect of half-folding the hexagons back (prior to any stay-stitching). Finger press the pleat; machine stitch up the crease towards the centre.

To prevent the threads unravelling, pull them through to the back and tie together, or reverse the machine stitching over the original line, or complete the line of sewing using a very small stitch length.

Figs. 14a & b

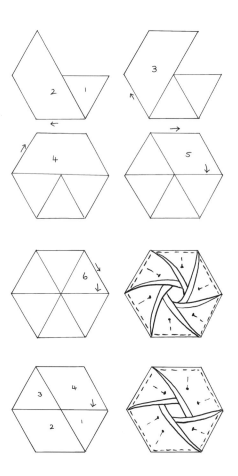

16

Lightly stuff the sections (Fig. 15), stay stitch to secure the edges and trim off excess. This was designed by Fay Purnell from the Quilt Room in Dorking, suffering her first workshop with me.

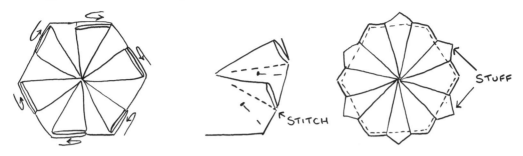

Fig. 15

Interlocking Rectangles

This is a little different from the others as the shape is not perfectly symmetrical, but it will interlock.

1. To make one block cut four rectangles of any size and colour. If you wish to be specific add the seam allowance to the basic size.

If using a fabric with a R/S and W/S, lay the rectangles all W/S up in a tidy pile (you have to be very systematic with the folding). There is no right or wrong side to calico but you must still be extra careful with the folding. Two rectangles are folded in half from the bottom left corner to the top right. The other two rectangles are folded in half from the top left to the bottom right corner (they do not fold evenly). Trim off the excess. Interleave as before (Fig. 16).

Fig. 16

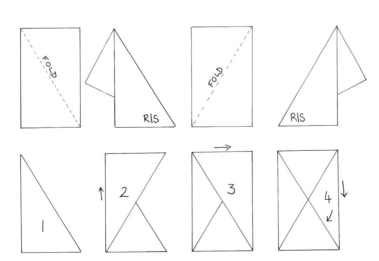

2. Pin all the layers very carefully before stay stitching round the outer edge. Roll the folds back and a diamond shape will appear in the centre (Fig. 17). The size and angles of the diamond are directly affected by the proportion of the sides of the rectangles.

(There is probably some amazing mathematical formula relating to the length of the opposite sides, amount of the roll back and the appearance of the central hole. Fibonacci is bound to come into the equation somewhere - more about him later.)

3. Complete the textured rectangle as with the squares and triangles.

Fig. 17

There is no real difficulty in making one rectangle, but the block will not pinwheel (rotate round at 90° on the same point) as the sides are not identical - pinwheels can only be created with identical sized and formed pieces. To make a block of four rectangles as in Fig. 18, just make four the same.

Fig. 18

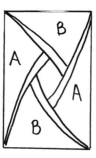

Fig. 19

If experimenting in colour with shades in specific places then be careful which way you fold the rectangles at the beginning (Fig. 19). The rectangles must be folded *in mirror images* of each other if colour A is to be on opposite sides; ditto with colour B.

Should you desire a mirror image (Fig. 20), reverse not only the direction of rotation but also the original folding. **Be very systematic.**

Fig. 20

It took me a long time to work out that everything had to be reversed. Two of the initial four rectangles still have to be folded from bottom left to top right; therefore to mirror image the block, these two rectangles are now folded top left to bottom right and vice versa with the other two. It does work (Fig. 20) if you are very systematic!

Developing the Interlocking Designs

Use of colour has been mentioned and can look most effective. Why not try the designs with coloured transparent materials? Then as the shapes interweave the colours will mix.

What about striped fabrics? Rolling back the stripes on the bias folds will add a further dimension to the designs.

Experiment with the texture of the material filling the space. Try some ruching or fine pin tucks or zip foot tucks. (See Textured Landscapes page 72 for method.)

Try making the Interlocking Squares in Fibonacci related sizes. This will really earn you loads of brownie points. (Fibonacci is from pages 55 - 61.)

Turn the Interlocked Equilateral Triangles over and appreciate that the reverse side has a different appearance. Whereas you had four sided shapes when you interleave as in the instructions, on the reverse side the shapes are three sided. Use a mixture of both sides in a design. Introduction of colour can produce some amazingly unusual blocks.

Explore the appearance of all kinds of Interlocked Hexagons all mixed in together. It would make an amazing wall-hanging.

What about the effect of Interlocking Diamonds? These have to be folded in two ways - one from side to side and the other from end to end (see Fig. 34a page 27), then you interweave as previously. Cut the shapes out with the grain line as indicated in Fig. 33 (page 26). The central shape is not quite as expected!

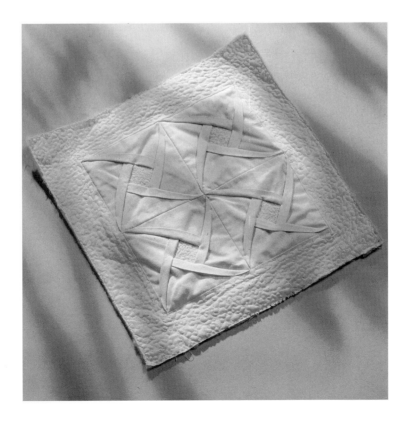

Corners

on Log Cabin

There is a book written on this particular method which I have not seen as yet. I first saw the design used on a quilt made by Karen Hellaby - the owner of Quilters Haven. It had been put on the bed where I was sleeping. Being of an inquisitive nature I had a thoroughly good look at the construction and on realising the natty technique involved began to ponder on 'What would happen if.....?'

I have to confess that somewhere in the quilt were several apple pips and at least one small coin. (When you construct a corner on the log cabin pattern the effect is produced by folding little squares in half then inserting these into the patchwork, because they are not stitched down on all sides a small pocket is formed.) As I wake early when sleeping in unfamiliar surroundings, one way of passing the time till breakfast is by sorting out the contents of my handbag and assuaging the pangs of hunger by munching apples. Gaily I tipped the mess out on to the quilt and some bits and pieces promptly slid into the little pockets. I am certain that several small coins were irretrievably lost in these pockets and certainly there was not the usual amount of apple pips left from the fruit. The more I shook the quilt the more these items must have shot from pocket to pocket. I only hope that no one spills any water on the quilt or a small tree may germinate. One's sins always find one out!

The whole clue to this new interpretation of this technique lies in the small squares which are folded in two across the diagonal (bias). If you have read the previous chapters or the last book you will remember that anything folded on the bias will roll back from the fold in an arc shape. So what happens if.........?

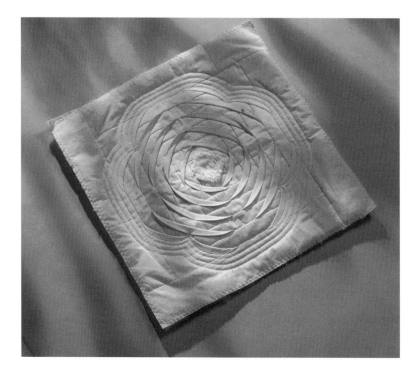

The original had all the corner sections cut from the same size squares; to make one 12"(30cm) finished block of this modified technique you need :-

3/4 x 1½"(3.5cm) strips approximately 45"(150cm) long
(cut strips across the fabric from selvedge to selvedge)
1 x 2½"(6cm) square (centre)
4 x 3"(7.5cm) squares, 4 x 3½"(9cm) squares,
4 x 4"(10.5cm) squares, 4 x 4½"(12cm) squares,
4 x 5"(13.5cm) squares.
(Each set of squares is increased by ½" or 1.5cm)

1. Frame the centre square with one of the 1½"(3.5cm) strips, using the basic Log Cabin sewing method (as shown in the diagrams). Attach to one side R/S's together, *use ¼"(.5cm) seam allowance,* fold back and trim flush with the centre square; now *working anti-clockwise* attach the strip to the next side, fold back and trim flush with centre square; attach to the third side, fold back and trim flush with centre square. Finally attach to the fourth side; fold back and trim flush with the first strip (Fig. 21). Press gently with all the seams pressed towards the outer edges.

2. Press all the sets of squares in half on the diagonal, R/S out. Select the first set - 4 x 3"(7.5cm). Place on the corners (Fig. 22). Tuck the last triangle under the first. Pin and stay stitch round the outer edge to stabilise the pieces (Fig. 23)

Fig. 21

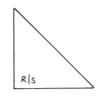
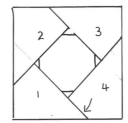
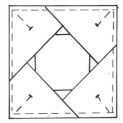

Figs. 22 & 23

3. Add more strips round the block (Fig. 24) using the same technique described in stage 1 . Try to start in the same place as before. Gently press all seams outwards.

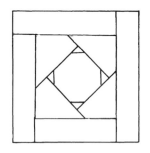

Fig. 24

4. Select the next sized set of squares, press and position as before (Fig. 25). Take care that they are parallel to the previous ones. Pin and stay stitch.

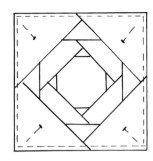

Fig. 25

Continue in this fashion until all the squares have been attached. They will only overlap in the first few rounds, because the squares are more spaced out as the block increases in size (Fig. 26).

**Check for accuracy -
keep the block as square as possible**

Fig. 26

5. The block should now measure 12½"(32cm) including the seam allowance - *12"(30cm) being the finished size*. (Deduct the seam allowances to obtain the finished size.) Add borders to frame the block. These could be attached as described on page 84 of **'Tucks Textures & Pleats'**, or use the Log Cabin method. (The only problem with the Log Cabin method is the size of the strips; there is always one short strip and one strip the full length of the block which gives an uneven appearance to the seams.) There is another method of attaching borders *using four equally sized strips*.

Decide on the width of the border - *remember to do all calculations based on the finished size*. Add the finished length of the block (12"/30cm) to the desired finished width of the border; this gives you the correct length of strip to cut. Now, add the seam allowances *on all sides* to both the length and the width measurements of the required strip.

i.e. Length of strip (block measurement):- 12"(30cm) + border width 3"(7.5cm)
= 15"(37.5cm)
Width of strip (border measurement):- 3"(7.5cm)
With seam allowances strip will measure
15"(37.5cm) + [S/A ¼"(.5cm) x 2] = 15½"(38.5cm) in length
3"(7.5cm) + [S/A ¼"(.5cm) x 2] = 3½"(8.5cm] in width.

<u>Cut FOUR strips this measurement.</u>
(**<u>Always</u>** cut strips from selvedge to selvedge across the material.)

(Cutting strips is much easier with a rotary cutter and ruler. For advice on cutters, rulers and the required board, see **'Tucks Textures & Pleats'**.)

Attach to the block by lining up the first strip with the base of the block. Commence stitching 2½"(7cm) down from the top of the block and sew to the bottom. Fold back and press gently. Line up the next strip with the outer edge of the border and the base of the block and sew. *Work anti-clockwise.*

Repeat with the next and the final strip. Flip the block over and complete the first seam (Fig. 27).

This method has seams evenly spaced and pin-wheeling round the block. Using this technique omits the two longer strips required in previous techniques as all the pieces are the same length and can be cut from a slightly less wide piece of cloth.

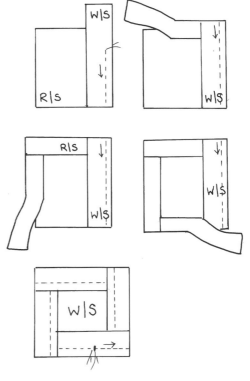

Fig. 27

6. Now that the borders are in place the folded edges of the squares can be rolled back. Place the entire block on to 2oz wadding/batting and cut roughly round. Pin the four corners through to the wadding. Roll back the folds and secure with a small stitch (Fig. 28). The entire length of the fold could be stitched down either by hand or machine. See Textured Landscapes chapter (page 75) for the blind hem stitch.

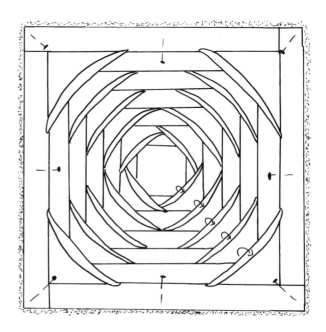

Fig. 28

Fig. 29

Experiment with differing amounts of rolling. Do all the edges of all the squares have to be rolled? Do they all have to be rolled back the same distance? Does the fold have to be rolled back in one piece?

If you catch the centre of the fold with a small stitch, then roll back both sides, a totally different effect will be achieved (Fig. 29).

Explore the effect of four blocks stitched together and a different colour inserted in the centre with the folded sides of the squares rolled over the raw edges of the insertion as in Fig. 30.

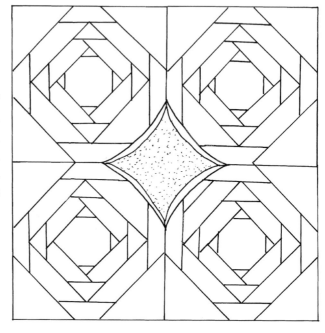

Fig. 30

Textured Hanging (25") with Ruched centre, Interlocked Shapes and 'Star Flower' inserts
framed with a padded bias strip; machine quilted (Jennie Rayment).

Corners on Log Cabin cushion (19″) with striped squares, Contrariwise Cathedral Window Mat and corduroy Scrip Bag (Jennie Rayment).

Shopping Bag (20″ x 15″) using a Fibonacci related design with striped Sculptured Sphere (Jennie Rayment).

Hexagon Box (12″) with Interlocking Triangles (Jennie Rayment).

Experiment with the Technique

1. Explore the use of colour by changing the colour of the central square or make the basic block from one colour and cut the squares out in a different colour. Make up the log cabin part of the block in different colours. Cut the initial strips in two colours; use one colour for the first and second strip round the block then the other colour for the third and fourth strips.

Why do the squares have to be **all the same colour?** Make the squares from two different coloured triangles stitched together; trim off excess seams; fold diagonally on the seam and attach as before. On rolling back the folded edge the reverse side of the square will show (Fig. 31).

Fig. 31

2. Texture the centre of the square. Replace the central section with a ruched square or when you have laid the block on to the wadding, embellish the centre with some machine or hand embroidery. What about some free machine quilting? See Interlocking Shapes chapter for the method.

3. Try striped material. If you cut the 1½"(3.5cm) strips from across (right-angles to selvedge) the fabric, the stripes will run both horizontally and vertically when you construct the Log Cabin part of the method. Cutting some strips down (parallel to selvedge) the material as well as across will keep all the stripes running in the same direction. To achieve this effect, the first and third strips are cut from the *horizontal strip* and the second and fourth are cut from the *vertical.*

Take care in the sewing and check more carefully for accuracy as the vertically cut strips lack the same amount of stretch as the others and can cause some distortion in the piecing.

Then go really mad and have the squares also cut from striped fabric; *watch how you fold them or some of the stripes will go the other way.*

4. Change the measurements and make a miniature one, or design a wall-hanging from different sized blocks and diverse measurements and colours.

5. Why not keep the folded squares all the same size or change them? Why not have every other round of squares a dissimilar size, larger or smaller?

6. Never make the Pineapple Log Cabin Patchwork again as the block is very similar to this type of patchwork and is constructed with a lot less effort!

Corners on Triangular Log Cabin

Explore the method with a 60° (equilateral) triangle (see page 14). The design is created with a series of **increasingly larger diamonds** that are folded in half, attached to the three corners and rolled back.

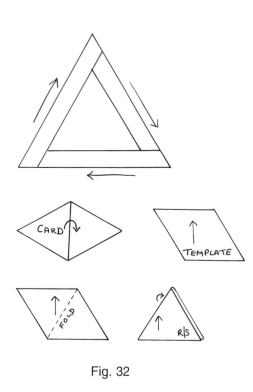

Fig. 32

1. Construct an equilateral triangle with 2″ (5cm) sides (see Interlocking Equilateral Triangles for method) - *add the seam allowances afterwards.* Make a template and cut the triangle out from the desired fabric. Cut 1½″(3.5cm) strips as before. Sew the strips round (Fig. 32).

Check the angle of the strip before you trim off, <u>open out and fold back</u> the strip then cut in line with last piece.

2. Using the same triangular template draw round on some card; flip over on one side and redraw a further triangle forming a diamond. Indicate the straight grain as in Fig. 32. Cut out three diamonds using this template - *watch the direction of the grain.* Fold in half re-forming a triangle and position on the edges of the Log Cabin block; pin and secure with stay stitching (Fig. 33).

3. Attach the next round of strips as in stage 1. *Watch the trimming!*

4. Using the same template as before draw round on the fabric *(draw on the W/S) and cut out ¼″(.5cm)* outside the drawn lines; use a Quilter's Quarter or measure with a ruler and draw the line. Make two more diamonds the same size. Fold in half on the bias to form triangles, and add to the block as in stage 2 (Fig. 32a). Ensure that all the triangles are parallel to the last set.

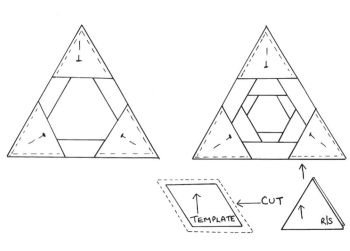

Figs. 33 & 33a

5. Add a further row of strips as in stage 1.

6. Using the same template draw round and **add ½"(1cm) to the drawn line** and cut out. Repeat to form two more diamonds. Fold in half; attach as before. Continue until the block is the desired size **adding an extra ¼"(.5cm)** to each succeeding round of triangles.

An alternative to using the same template would be to make individual folded diamonds (triangles) for each round of Log Cabin. If you wish to do this, then the block must be drawn to scale on either imperial (inches) or metric (centimetres) graph paper, drawing in the triangles and adding the seam allowances to each one separately - *remember, that the triangle in the scale drawing is really a folded diamond and there is no seam allowance on the inner edge*. The previously described method is faster but not quite so accurate.

If you made six the same size then these could be pieced together to form a hexagon (Fig. 34)! Open as many seams as possible and/or cut part of the underside of the attached diamond to reduce to reduce some of the bulk. When joining the six triangles together, stitch into pairs then stitch the pairs together matching the seam lines. Start sewing from the centre; begin on the stitched lines and sew to the end of the seam. None of the seams should be joined at the very centre to ensure that they can pivot round and enable the block to lie flat. This may leave a small hole which can be stitched by hand.

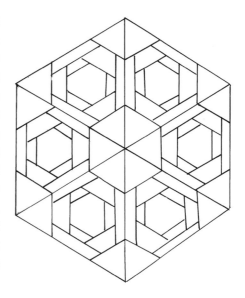

Fig. 34

Explore Further Ideas

Try the possibilities with other shapes of Log Cabin. It can be constructed with diamond shaped designs or even hexagonal based Log Cabin. Using a diamond shaped pattern the folded shapes which will also be diamonds are folded in two ways. Two are folded across the width, two across the length. The grain line for cutting is the same as for the Triangular technique. With the hexagon based design the folded shapes will be hexagons. Care must be taken to fold the pieces across the bias edge before attaching.

The combinations of colour, shape and texture are endless, but do remember not to eat apples in bed!

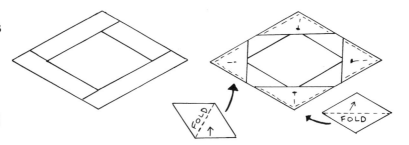

Contrariwise

Cathedral Windows

(Or the J.R. version.)

This section was developed on one of those days when the brain was actually working. The poor old grey cell had been galvanised into action and was roaring round at well over the speed limit, pinging off the inner confines of the skull, and bouncing with gay abandon. Who is Gay Abandon?

Sadly this state of affairs did not last and as the sun sank slowly in the west so did the grey cell. I used to think that I had several of these things then the truth dawned - there was only a solitary one! Now I am aware that this one must have gone too because, having had my head x-rayed some weeks ago, there was no trace of anything . The skull was totally empty! Thank goodness I had devised this notion before the system collapsed. You may now nod sagely and think 'Yes, that explains everything, just an empty space between Rayment's ears'.

Does this really matter?

Now I will be serious. Cathedral Window is a type of folded patchwork. The name is derived from the appearance of the patch. On joining two blocks a space (window) is created which can contain a further scrap of material and the edges of the space will roll over the scrap framing it - not unlike a round church window. This is a completely new interpretation based on the traditional construction method which develops into something completely different. It can be twiddled, rolled and nipped. You can squash it or even create three dimensional ones ranging in size from Christmas decorations to a Bread Basket for the barbecue - is there no end to the woman's imagination?

Method - You need a 20"(50cm) square of cotton fabric - calico looks good and it's cheap.

1. Fold in half R/S together; using ¼"(.5cm) seam sew up the sides making a bag. Open and bring the sides to the middle, matching and opening seams. Sew along the raw edge; **leave a gap** and sew the remaining section (Fig. 35).

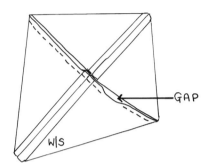

Fig. 35

2. Cut the corners off; clip the centre seams; turn R/S out through the gap (bet you didn't leave a big enough one); close the hole with slip stitch but do not stitch into the underneath layer. (This is not totally necessary - only for pernickety people!)

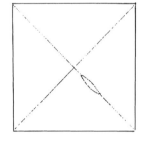

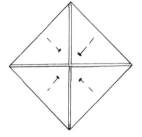

Fig. 36

3. Fold the corners to the centre; pin carefully then press gently (Fig. 36). (The points should meet but may need a gentle manipulation - don't we all!). Press the square very carefully - *don't stretch the sides*.

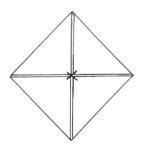

4. By hand link these points closely together with a cross stitch (Fig. 37). They do not overlap, merely touch.

Fig. 37

Do not stitch through to the under-layer - only stitch the points to themselves.

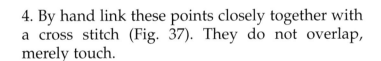

Fig. 38

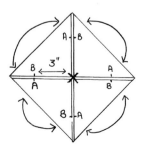

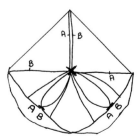

5. Measure 3"(7.5cm) from the centre to points A and B (Fig. 38). Bring A and B together and stitch lightly by hand *through the edges of the fold only, not all the layers.* (This stitching will probably be removed later.) Repeat on all four sections.

6. Carefully arrange the folds as in Fig. 39. They will all touch and lie flat although it may need a little manipulation. Some fabrics have to be persuaded more than others. Pin the folds down and secure the junction C with a tiny stitch. Whether you choose to stitch through all the layers or not depends on the final creation. The previous light stitching between A and B may now be removed.

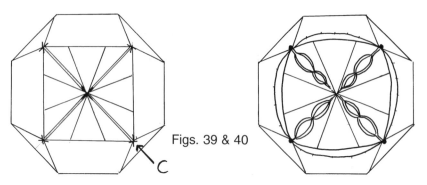

Figs. 39 & 40

As with so many textural creations there are lots of ways to develop the design.

a. Make interesting textural element to the central section by rolling back the edges and catching down with a tiny hand stitch (Fig. 40 & Fig. 41). Add a bead or two when you sew.

b. Roll back the folds on the outer edges (Fig. 40) and secure by hand stitching or use the blind hem stitch on the machine (see page 75 for details). It is your choice whether you sew through all the layers or just the top one. Try catching the mid-point of the fold and then rolling back as in Fig. 41.

c. Add a further colour by cutting round the outline and laying the fabric inside; then roll back as before. Insert more colour into the folds of the central section; roll back to reveal the extra shade.

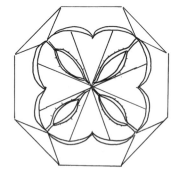

d. Try inserting a textured sample such as ruching or pin-tucks (see 'Tucks Textures & Pleats')

Fig. 41

e. Make several and link together with squares of either textured material or another colour.

f. Experiment with stripes: the result can be migraine-making.

g. Make a small one and convert into an ornament. Stitch at C as in Stage 6 but not through to the base layer - only the top two folds to the next layer. Then very carefully pull it out. The best ornaments are made with stiffer fabric. Please do not ask what you can do with it - that I shall leave to your imagination! (See photograph.)

For a further idea why not use the technique to make a Bread Basket?

A Bread Basket

A truly neat little basket for the bread at the chic dinner party or to embellish the barbecue table. Astonish your friends with this natty number! Did you know that

'Where guests at a gathering are well-acquainted,
they eat 20% more than they otherwise would'
Edgar Watson Howe - Country Town Sayings (1911)

Perhaps you should make two! You need:-

24½"(62cm) sq for basket + 4 x [12"(30cm) x 1¼"(3cm)] strips
2 x 9½"(24cm) sqs of fabric for the base
Approx 10"(25cm) sq of 2oz wadding/batting + 8½"(21cm) sq of pelmet vilene

1. Make the tabs out of the strips. Fold long sides to middle and press; refold in half along the long edges and press again (R/S out). Tuck in one end of each tab to avoid a raw end. Carefully stitch along the very edge of both sides. Alternatively try a Rouleau needle/loop turner to turn the tabs. (May be a little awkward with such a fine strip of material.) **Start stitching at the untucked end; help machine as it stitches over the thicker tucked end. (Reducing the stitch length initially will prevent threads unravelling.)**

2. Taking the large square, mark the centres of all the sides. Stitch the tabs on, keeping the sewing within the seam allowance. Pin the loose ends firmly to the square (Fig. 42).

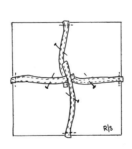

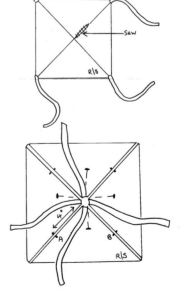

3. Continue with the construction as in stage 1 - 3 on page 29. A and B are measured 4"(10cm) from the centre.

Fig. 42

Fig. 43

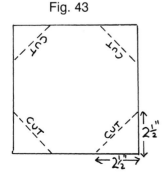

4. Make the base to the basket with the 8½"(21cm) pelmet vilene square. Measure 2½"(7cm) from all corners, rule a line from these points and cut through line (forms an octagon).

Construct a sandwich of wadding, both fabric squares R/S together, and pelmet vilene; pin well. Stitch round all the layers keeping as close to the vilene as possible (Fig. 44). **Leave one side un-stitched.** Trim off excess and turn R/S out through the gap. Close the opening with a slip stitch.

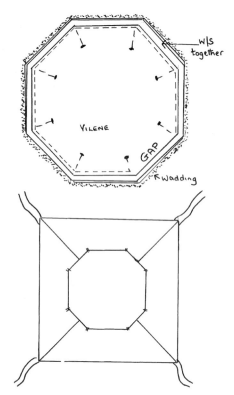

5. Remove the pins from the main square and position the base as in Fig. 44. Secure the corners of the base by hand stitching through all the layers. Refold the flaps as before.

Fig. 45

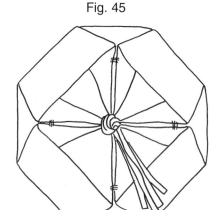

Fig. 44

6. Measure 4"(10cm) from the centre to points A and B (see Fig. 38) and stitch **firmly**. Carefully arrange the folds and flatten as in stage 5 page 29. Tie the tabs together in a knot (Fig. 45). Remove the pins and lift the basket by the tabs.

Open the side folds and - **Hey Presto! - a breadbasket.** Make a matching table cloth and fringed napkins (see page 67 of **'Tucks Textures and Pleats'**). Go totally O.T.T. with mats and napkin rings as well. (See photograph.)

Silly Idea for a Napkin Ring

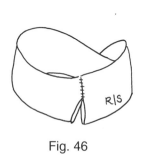

Fig. 46

Cut a strip of fabric approximately 14"(35cm) long x 4½"(12cm) wide. With R/S together, stitch along the edges making a tube; turn R/S out. Twist the band before joining the ends to form a circle. Carefully sew the raw ends together but leave a gap to thread some wide elastic through (Fig. 45). Cut 7"(18cm) elastic; thread through - *remember to pin one end on to the fabric so it will not pull out.* Sew the ends of the elastic firmly; close the gap with small hand stitches. Now you will have a scrunchy napkin ring.

Last instruction: Lay the table, invite the guests for supper or have a romantic meal under the starlit sky with a loved one! The guests will probably spill wine on the cloth and not notice the table setting, or the weather will be foul, pouring with rain and freezing cold (the Green-house Effect). I am the eternal optimist!

Rectangular Method

This requires a very different template to the square version. The pattern can be found in several books on Cathedral Windows; one of the best is 'Through the Window' by Lynn Edwards.

Try and make your own.

Template for Rectangular Cathedral Windows

You need a large sheet of paper, pair of compasses*, pencil and ruler. (*Henceforth to be known as a compass!)

1. Draw a rectangle the required finished size. To demonstrate the technique the rectangle will be 3"(8cm - rounded up) x 6"(16cm). Label the corners ABCD clockwise starting from top left. Find the centre either by drawing the diagonals or by measuring. Draw the central horizontal and vertical lines (Fig. 47). Label (as in diagram) XZYW and mark centre O.

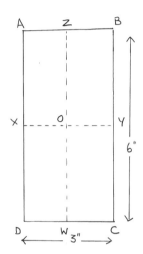

Fig. 47

2. Extend X to E [same length as XO - 1½"(4cm)], repeat with OY to F. Extend Z to G [same length as ZO - 3"(8cm)], repeat with OW to H (Fig. 48).

   EO =3"(8cm), FO = 3"(8cm),.
   GO = 6"(16cm), HO = 6"(16cm).

Fig. 48

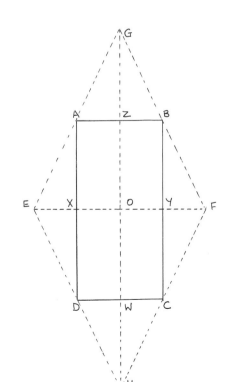

Join points GE, GF, HE, HF; the lines will all touch points ABCD - if not, you have gone wrong!

33

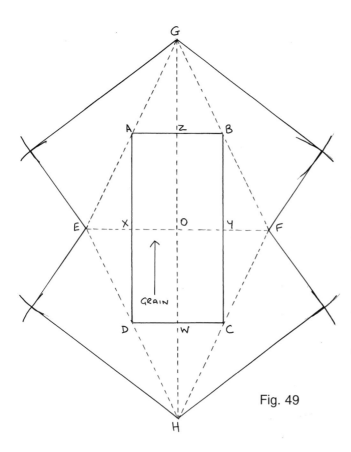

3. Add triangles to the four sides as in the diagram. Place the compass point at H, stretch the compass to O, and draw a large faint arc outside the rectangle on both sides. Repeat at point G. Place compass point on E and stretch the compass to O, draw an arc on each side crossing through the others. Repeat at F (Fig. 49). Join all the points.

Finally add ¼"(.5cm) seam allowance all round; add the grain line and relax.

Fig. 49

Method

Trace off the template and either stick this on to a large sheet of card or use template plastic and trace through.

1. Cut out one shape in material. Fold in half, R/S together (Fig. 50). Stitch the long sides using the normal seam allowance. Pull apart; match and open seams; sew across; leave a gap then complete the stitching. It is a good idea to clip the seams before turning R/S out through the gap. Very carefully poke the corners out and slip stitch the hole. Continue as in stages 3 - 4 on page 29.

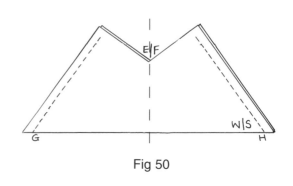

Fig 50

2. Measure approximately 2/3rds down the sides as before and link together with a small hand stitch. Carefully arrange the folds. This new block can now be manipulated in exactly the same manner as described on page 30.

Try linking the shapes together as in the picture with a central section of ruching. Explore the effect of inserting a different fabric in this space and tucking raw edges under the folds (Fig. 51).

Fig. 51

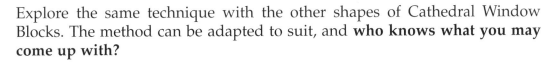

As these are rectangles they can be fitted in two ways. Experiment with the design.

Make a panel for the wall or use as an appliqué for a quilt block. Embellish with beads and sequins etc. Add a small bead under the central folds to create a three dimensional appearance.

Explore the same technique with the other shapes of Cathedral Window Blocks. The method can be adapted to suit, and **who knows what you may come up with?**

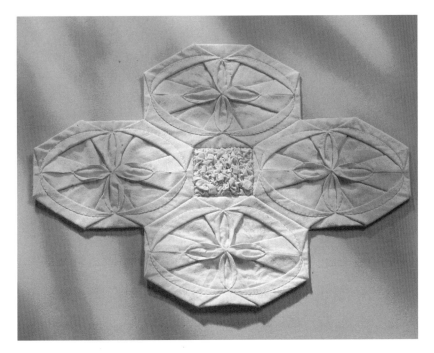

Sculptured

Spheres

It was the week before Christmas and at the end of a heavy day's work we had repaired to the local hostelry for a quick pint or two. Whilst we were sat sitting there in the dim, dark gloom I noticed some of the Christmas decorations hanging above our heads. Ah - a new design idea! Forget the food, allow the mouth to fall open and cogitate about the hows, whys, wherefores and possibilities. I could see a real neat idea for a textured ball. A large, highly coloured, glittering paper globe was hanging from the rafters. I was sure that this could be translated into material.

It must have been very irritating for my companion to have the virtues of the dangling ornaments extolled at length when all he wished to talk about was world affairs and other such erudite matters. How can one conduct a serious conversation with someone who is waxing lyrical about the angle of the dangle, the degree of the design, the area of the circumference, and going on about duodecahedrons, Archimedes and good old Pythagoras to boot? I could see his eyes glazing over and that look of resignation as I waffled on. People can get really bored with one's obsessional interest with 'nipping and tucking'.

So from that inauspicious beginning sprang 'Sculptured Spheres'. They were nearly called 'P.O.W. Balls' as the pub (hostelry) was the 'Prince of Wales'; on reflection this was not the best name. When writing anything these days it is terribly important to be politically correct and ensure that you do not offend anyone at all. One must ensure that everything is defined carefully as the last thing one would ever want to do would be to cause any offence, and even land up with a libel/slander suit (can never remember which one is which).

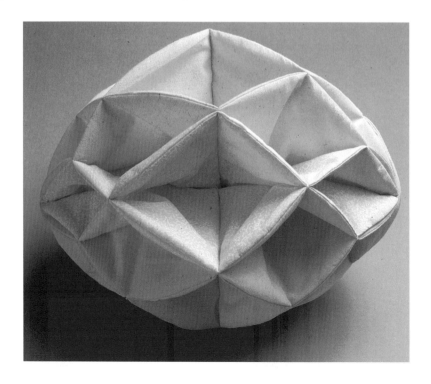

The design potential of these 'Spheres' is extensive as you can link 6 - 8 circles together at various angles to create different effects. In miniature, they could be used for Christmas Tree decorations, earrings or mobiles; in a larger size they could be interesting as children's toys or as fascinating 'objets d'art'. We all need to have dust collectors and these will be highly effective as an accumulator of fluff, dirt and detritus. Gosh it all sounds so attractive!!

Padded Sculptured Spheres

You need :-

6 x 8"(20cm) circles in two colours of cotton
fabric (12 in total) although you could try
any combination of colours
¼ yd (mtr) 2oz wadding/batting or similar
(60"/150cm wide)
Toning thread
(Measurements include seam allowances.)

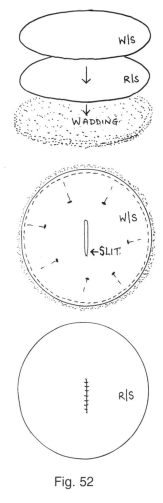

1. Divide the circles into pairs containing one of each colour; *lay R/S together*. Cut 6 circles of wadding/batting a little larger than the 8"(20cm) circle. Place fabric circles on to wadding and pin. Stitch round the outer edge by hand or machine with ¼"(.5cm) seam allowance. Trim any excess wadding/batting.

2. Fold the circles in half and carefully slit a small hole in the centre of the fold. Turn the circle (inside out) through the slit - R/S out; close the slit with a small hand stitch (Fig. 52).

Fig. 52

Fig 53

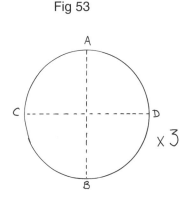

3. Fold **3** of the circles in half keeping the same coloured side on the outside; lightly draw the central line (A/B). Refold in half (C/D) and draw a further line. There will now be two lines crossing at right-angles drawn on one side (Fig. 53).

4. Place one of these drawn-on circles on to one of the remaining padded shapes (matching colours). Pin together; stitch down the lines. Start with a small machine stitch then increase the stitch length until you reach the end, then decrease the stitch length again. This will help to prevent the threads unravelling. If sewing by hand then follow the same procedure. Repeat twice more with the rest of the circles. There will be now 3 pairs of circles sewn A/B and C/D (Fig. 54).

Fig. 54

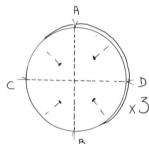

5. Take one of the pairs and rule a line F/G at 45° to AB as in Fig. 55. Use a protractor to measure accurately, or fold in half matching the stitching lines and firmly finger press; then rule the line.

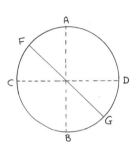
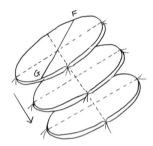
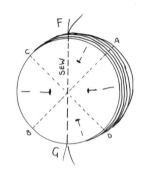

Fig. 55

6. Place this set directly on top of the other two sets, matching the seam lines (Fig. 55). The next line of stitch may require a thicker machine or hand needle (90/100 machine needle). Stitch down the last ruled line (F/G) thus joining all the circles together. (They will fan out from this line of stitching to form a sphere.)

7. Mark with a pin or pencil dot the mid point X and Y between A/D and C/B on all six circles. By hand link X to Y together in pairs; join the opposite sides as in Fig. 56.

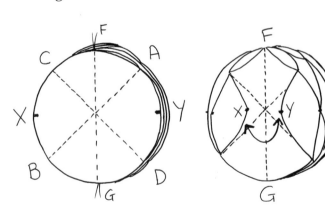
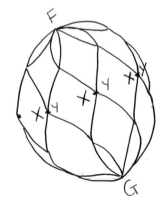

Fig. 56

Why not add a bead or link the edges together with a quilting tie? How about a sequin or small tassel (but do remember the age of the recipient)? It would not be advisable to give small children anything that they could inadvertently swallow. Experiment with marking more subdivisions and linking together.

Interlocked Hexagons (16″ square) mounted on board
(Jennie Rayment).

Textured Waistcoat with panel of 'Crossing over the Tucks' and Woven
Scrip Bag (Jennie Rayment).

Contrariwise Cathedral Window Hanging (32″ x 20″) with 'Star
Flower' centre and inserts of traditional Cathedral Window squares
(Jennie Rayment).

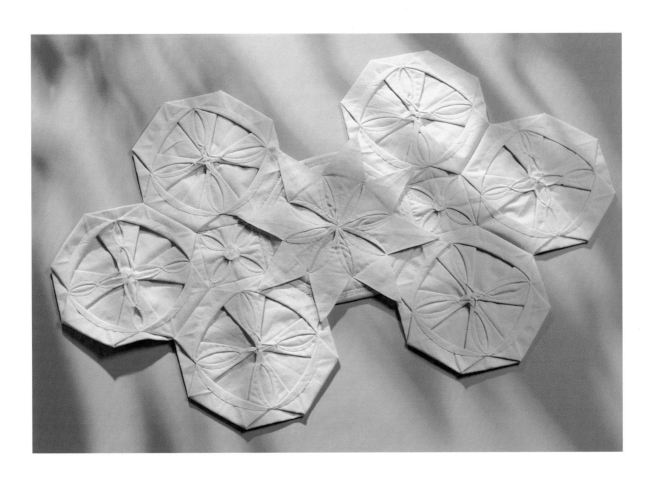

Textured Landscape (10″ x 15″) with microwaved dyed shades and other special dyed effects (Jennie Rayment).

Bolster cushion (18″ x 8″) featuring Interlocked Rectangles with pin-tucked centres (Jennie Rayment).

Square Sculptured Sphere with miniature 45° and 60° spheres in silver and gold metallic fabric (Jennie Rayment).

Christmas Decorations

You need:-

Small quantity of 'Bondaweb' or 'Heat 'n Bond' or a similar fabric fusible glue web.
Small quantity of light-weight fusible interfacing such as 'Vilene'.
Silver and/or gold metallic material.
Sequins, beads, metallic threads for decoration.

I found the fusible interfacing to be useful as it stiffened the metallic fabric although it can be difficult to bond to the material. Use of a damp cloth helped when pressing.

Method

1. Press the fusible interfacing to the back of both metallic fabrics. Take care not to damage the material. Re-pressing from the R/S with a damp cloth did aid the removal of any creases.

Make sure that you attach the glued side to the fabric not the iron.
You will not be a happy bunny if you get it wrong!

2. Following the manufacturer's instructions iron the fusible glue web on to the back of one of the metallic fabrics. 'Bondaweb' usually needs a hot iron; 'Heat 'n Bond' normally requires a cool iron.

Do not remove the backing paper yet.

Press again from the R/S to ensure that the web is firmly attached to the material.

3. Now peel off the backing paper and lay the two fabrics W/S together. Press well. Use a damp cloth between the fabric and the iron to prevent any damage.

4. Cut six circles 3½"(9cm) from the bonded fabric. Make a circular template and draw round or use a compass to draw circles on the material. For speed use a cup or similar; the final size of the circles is not critical.

5. Divide the circles into pairs matching the colours on the inside. Draw the central line A/B as in Fig. 53 on one side and stitch the pairs of circles down the central line.

6. Draw C/D on one set of circles (Fig. 53). Place the stitched pairs on top of each other matching the stitched line and sew together following C/D. Use a metallic thread to sew with and leave long dangling ends as you start sewing. (The sphere can be hung from these threads.) This is a speedier way than the previous method but you will have more sections to link with hand stitching. (Developed by Lynette Harris of Hailsham.)

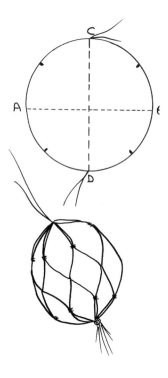

7. Mark with pencil or pin the midpoints between A/C:A/D:C/B:B/D. Link the sections together as before (Fig. 57) with a small hand stitch. Attach beads, sequins or small tassels. Try leaving long thread ends for extra decoration.

Change the size, colours and decoration. Make dozens for a fabulous Christmas tree. Look really festive with very tiny ones for ear-rings!

Fig. 57

Although the shape begins with circles the finished result may well be ovoid in appearance. This can be improved by making eight circles to begin with and having four sets to stitch together as described, but you may find the extra layers prove too thick to stitch through.

Further Ideas with Sculptured Spheres

Make more sections by changing the angle of stitching. Try 60°. Sew pairs of circles together on the initial A/B line; place protractor in centre; measure 60°; draw C/D (Fig. 58); stitch along C/D line. Re-draw E/F (60°) from A/B on one set only; sew all sets together on E/F line (Fig. 59). Link mid points of E/C and D/F by hand as before.

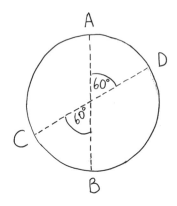

Fig. 58

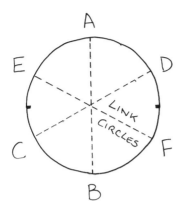

Fig. 59

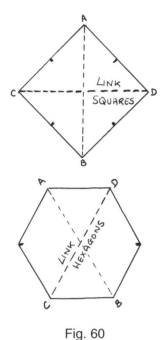

Fig. 60

Try the idea with squares linked together. Using the same technique sew A/B and C/D; mark mid-points; stitch together by hand (Fig. 60).

Experiment with different angles, shapes, lines and designs. Try oval 'Spheres' or will it work in equilateral (60°) triangles? (It does but you will really have to think hard and no alcohol until you have cracked the idea!)

What about stripes or directional designs? Investigate the scintillating appearance of vibrant colours, observe the juxtaposition and counterbalance of diametrically opposed tints, tones and shades - if you can understand that you are a better man than I, Gunga Din! For us of the lower orders merely combine the spectrum in a multi-faceted, many-hued 'Sculptured Sphere'.

**Goodness me!
What a lot of choices!!**

Textural Titbits

This chapter is a compilation of all sorts of ideas with texture. In the last book there were several techniques fairly basically described, so here is an extended look at some of those ideas. The more I teach the more I learn, and it never ceases to amaze me how many different things can be created from one elementary principle. Quite frequently a new interpretation will arise from a 'mistake'. You will remember the Rayment adage that 'mistakes do not matter - the result is just a little different'. The only real errors are caused by complete carelessness such as cutting out the wrong sizes or colours or maybe even cutting on the bias (cross) when it should have been straight grain. But will it really matter? No, probably not, although the final creation might not be completely square or lie totally flat; however you can nearly always cut a bit off or quilt heavily to remove the lumps and bumps! We do waste a lot of energy in trying to be perfect and sometimes in the cause of perfection miss that most exciting and innovative idea. Most things are nearly always rescuable if only one can relax and accept a different view of matters, and add a covered button or one or two extra tucks to sort things out. Why isn't life so easy?

Moving on from this homespun philosophy to the chapter, there are various different sections from 'Crossing over the Tucks' to a variation on 'Triangle Cornets' (page 52 of **'Tucks Textures & Pleats'**) and a fuller explanation of the 'Tucked Circle'.

Crossing over the Tucks

This is a method of constructing large tucks running diagonally across the material which are then ironed flat and the pleats manipulated. The method described here is a little different from the one in the previous book, giving you slightly less tucks to play with, but the scope for creativity is the same.

Method

1. Cut 18"(45cm) square of cotton material. Mark the midpoints of all the sides *on the R/S*. Fold in half diagonally *with R/S on the outside* matching up the marks. Sew 1"(2.5cm) seam parallel to the diagonal fold. Refold **exactly** on the other marks (Fig. 62); stitch another seam 1"(2.5cm) from this fold. Repeat with the other sets of marks. There will now be three large tucks running diagonally across the square.

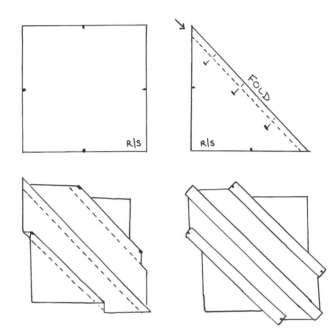

Fig. 62

2. Press the tucks flat ensuring that the tuck is lying evenly either side of the seam; inserting a thin ruler or 'Bias Bar' in the tuck or wiggling a large knitting needle from side to side will help to flatten it more easily. (Bias Bars are different sized strips of plastic or metal often used to create bias binding for 'Celtic' type designs. You can purchase Bias Bars in many Quilting shops. Both types are heat proof and can be ironed over.) The tucks now resemble box pleats running diagonally across a diamond (Fig. 62).

3. Repeat the entire operation from the opposite sides using the same seam allowance.

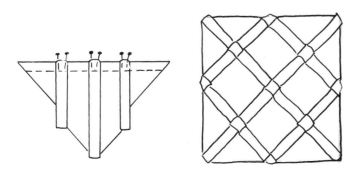

Fold exactly on the marks, *do not try to unfold the previous tuck - have faith!* Press again to flatten the tucks (Fig. 64). Magically the fabric will square up again with a lattice of tucks and will measure approximately 12"(30cm).

Figs. 63 & 64

4. Now for some fun. Cut a piece of 2oz wadding/batting slightly larger that the finished piece. Pin tucked sample on to the wadding and begin to play.

a. Gather up the centre knot with three small stitches or more if desired. If you bring the needle up through the top layer of the material only, it will ruche more easily. This makes an interesting scrunched bow. You could add a bead or small button. Catching (tacking U.S.A.) the thread through all the layers will secure the 'bow' to the base a little better (Fig. 65).

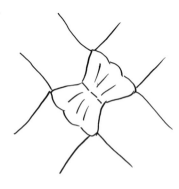

Fig. 65

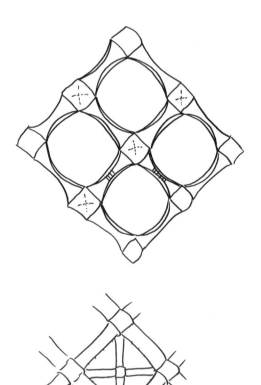

b. Roll the tucks together and anchor with an upright bar tack, or catch flat through all layers for a different effect. Twist one side of the tucks only, producing a curved appearance. Hold the edge of the tuck down with hand stitching or use the blind hem stitch (see page 75 for further details).

c. Insert a contrasting coloured piece of fabric. Place this underneath the larger tucks and secure by stitching along the original set of tucks.

Explore the effect of inserting a small panel of one 'Crossed over Tuck'. Make a tiny one from a 5"(12cm) square with a ½"(1cm) flattened tuck from each side (Fig. 66).

Fig. 66

From such humble beginnings many textural designs can grow.

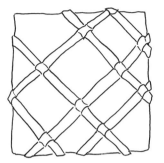

Why not try more tucks? Position the initial tucks at different intervals forming rectangles instead of squares in the spaces. Experiment with tucks over tucks at differing angles. There is no reason why you can't tuck at right-angles or at sixty degrees or at any angle. You could cross tucks over in a triangle.

How about alternating the size of the original seam and having large tucks and smaller ones?

Experiment with one small tuck on top of another one. Do this by stitching a small seam across the material then stitch a much larger one. Press both the small tuck and the large tuck flat together. This produces one tiny flattened tuck on top of another larger one making double the effect!

It is possible to make a strip of this technique for use as a border of a quilt, wall-hanging or insert into a garment. Simply cut a strip of any width and mark out in squares. Then make the first set of tucks, press and repeat the method from the opposite direction (Fig. 67).

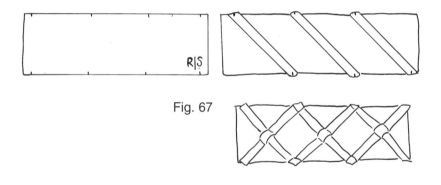

Fig. 67

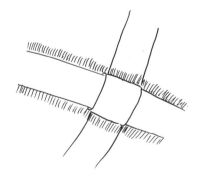

Finally add some fringing to the design. Rip thin strips of fabric and attach to the original seams of the second set of tucks. (You can add fringing to both sets of tucks but it becomes very bulky.) If you rip a wide enough section then you will have double the fringed appearance.

So you can see the possibilities of this very elementary technique are endless and you will find many more ideas.

In 'Tucks Textures & Pleats' there were instructions for 'The Triangle Cornet' which consisted of a sewn fabric triangle inserted in a seam then manipulated. The crucial part of this design was to stitch the seam down one specific side of the basic triangle. You **had** to sew down the bias edge. Occasionally when I teach this effect, there are odd bods who misunderstand and stitch the wrong side (straight-grained side of triangle). The result is not quite the same as the original but I think preferable. Sadly a seam marred the finished creation, so I have revamped the design and here it is:-

Triangle Cornet (Mark 2) or the 'Star Flower'

In addition to being a new interpretation the textural inserts are placed close to the centre so that all the points meet in the middle. This is not the easiest thing to do but with care it is perfectly possible *providing you follow the instructions carefully paying especial attention to the diagrams.* If you don't succeed there is always a covered button!

1. Cut from *bias* grain 8 x 6"(15cm) squares to make the textural insertions. These squares are inserted into 4 x 9½"(24cm) squares (cut on the normal straight grain). Measurements include the seam allowance.

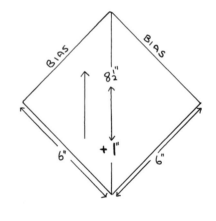

The measurement for the second set of squares must equal the diagonal of the first set plus 1"(2.5cm). The textural insertion increases in length when manipulated, consequently the squares into which it is inserted have to be considerably larger.

2. Fold the bias squares in half (R/S together) on the diagonal; sew one edge using ¼"(.5cm) seam. Clip off point; turn R/S out; gently poke out the point and seal the opening with a tack/baste; keep stitching close to the edges (Fig. 68). These sealed triangles will now be inserted (sandwiched) in each of the eight seams of the design so we will refer to them as 'sandwiches'.

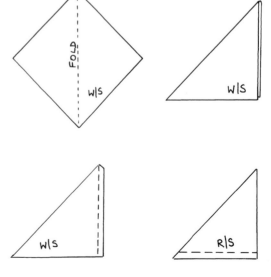

Fig. 68

3. Divide the second set of squares in half on the diagonal forming 8 triangles. Taking 2 of these triangles place one 'sandwich' on the bias edge, aligning the raw edges to ensure that the point is ⅜"(1cm) from the top. Pin in place. Position the remaining triangle on top; stitch a ⅜"(1cm) seam down the bias edge (Fig. 69). This 'sandwich' is now inserted diagonally in the square. Lightly press the seam open taking care not to crease the 'sandwich'. Repeat the instructions three more times making four squares with 'sandwiches' in them. There are still four 'sandwiches' remaining.

Should your sample fail to resemble the diagram just twist the 'sandwich' over - the textural insertion can lie on either side of the seam.

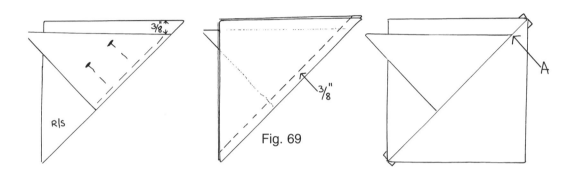

Fig. 69

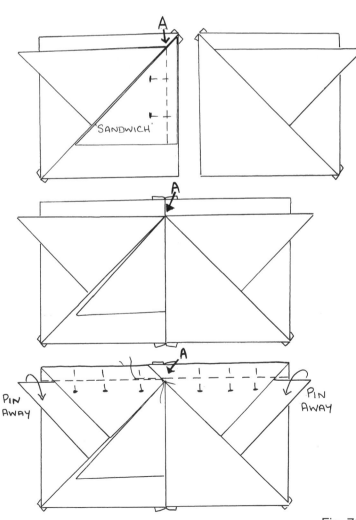

Fig. 71

4. Take two of these squares and one 'sandwich'; place the shape as shown in Fig. 70, pin and tack/baste to prevent movement. Lay the next square on top matching the points at A (R/S together); stitch down the side using ⅜"(1cm) seam. Gently press the seam open as above. Repeat: there are now two sets of squares with three textural inserts and there are still two 'sandwiches' left. *Pin shapes to the centre or they will 'catch' in the final seam.*

Fig. 70

5. Lay the last pair exactly as shown in the diagram (Fig. 71) on one of these sets. *Overlap at A.* Pin well, tack/baste to secure. Start at the centre sewing to one end, then reverse work and complete the line.

47

6. Take the second set of squares and place R/S together, lining all the A points in the centre; pin, tack/baste if preferred; sew this last seam (Fig. 72). Press the seams open trimming any excess bulk if desired. Open out. Manipulate the shapes by gently pulling the sides apart, thus extending the width and making the 'sandwich' easy to flatten (Fig. 72a).

Fig. 72

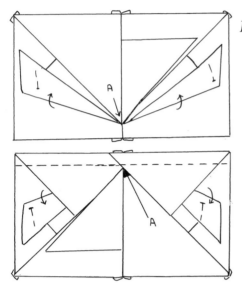

P.S. Covered buttons are really effective!

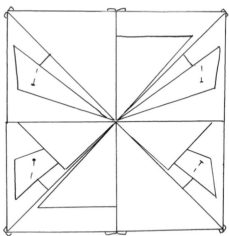

Developing the Design

Experiment with rolling and twisting the edges. Manipulate the flaps back and forth or fold over. Add beads or tassels to the points.

Leave the 'sandwiches' lying flat (unopened); insert a 'Prairie Point' or a 'Somerset Patch'; roll the edges of the 'sandwich'.

Insert the 'sandwich' into any seam. Have six in a hexagonal format; four in between squares or rectangles. Link side by side or in a row (end to end) for a border or as a textural insertion in a garment.

It's amazing what can be done with a 'mistake'.

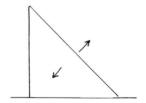

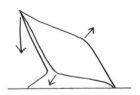

Fig 72a

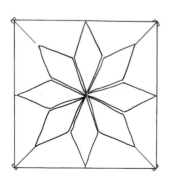

48

Tucked-up Circles

At the end of the second chapter of **'Tucks Textures & Pleats'** there was a short description of how to tuck up a circle. The first publication was intended to be an ideas and design manual with basic principles and methods followed by suggestions for development; but many people have asked for more information on this technique and for precise directions

Previously the method was given for marking up the circle in 9° sections. These latest instructions describe how to mark the circle at 10° intervals. It is possible to use any equal division of 360° that you care to choose, such as 12°, 15°, 18° or 20° etc. (360 must be divisible evenly). A tuck is formed on every mark: consequently 360° ÷ 10° = 36 - forms 36 tucks. Therefore if you select 12° intervals (360° ÷ 12° = 30) there will be only 30 tucks.

The reason for this change is of practical necessity; most of the mathematical instruments that we all possess are not very accurate nor very clearly printed and it easier to see the larger 10° divisions such as 60° than 54° for instance. (In addition not every one knows their '9 times' table!)

<u>Method</u>

You need:-

¾ yard/metre (approx) calico or similar material
Compass, protractor and long ruler.
(Seam allowances are included in the measurements.)

1. Rip out a 31"(79cm) square. Fold in half and half again. Carefully refold on the diagonal (Fig. 73). To be really accurate, fold one half to the front and the other to the back. Press gently.

Check that you have folded this correctly - the corners ABCD should be opposite the centre. Failure to fold correctly can end in disaster resulting in 4 x ¼ circles, not a whole one!

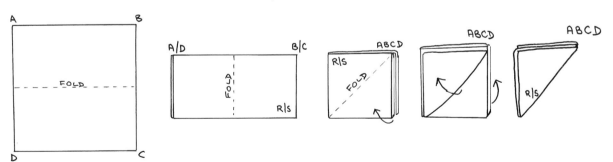

Fig. 73

Measure 15"(38cm) from the centre A along one side; mark. Repeat this measurement several times forming an arc across the material (Fig. 74). Pin layers together either side of the mark; cut carefully along the arc. This will form a circle 30"(76cm) wide. (Try this technique for cutting any large circles such as circular table-cloths.)

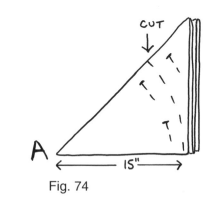

Fig. 74

2. Draw a cross (North/South, West/East) in the centre. Insert the point of the compass in the centre of cross and draw 9"(23cm) diameter circle. Set compass at 4½"(11.5cm). Placing protractor on this cross *(check the midpoint of the protractor is aligned with the cross)*, mark all the 10° intervals (Fig. 75). Reverse protractor to mark the lower half.

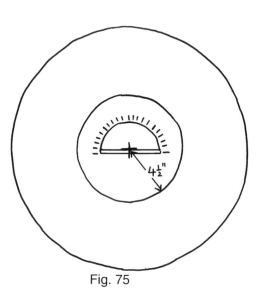

Fig. 75

3. Line up the ruler with the centre cross and one of the degree dots; mark the outside of the inner circle and the inside of the outer circle (Fig. 76). Put a small cross beside these first two lines; this will be the starting point. Systematically work your way round, taking care to be accurate. Taping the circle flat to the table may help to keep it smooth.

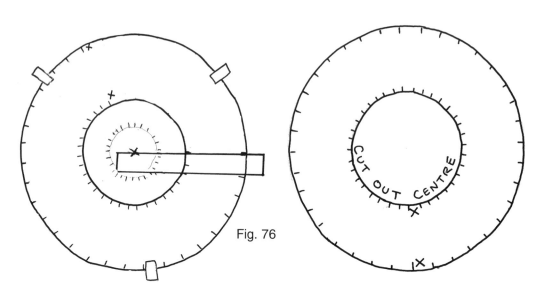

Fig. 76

50

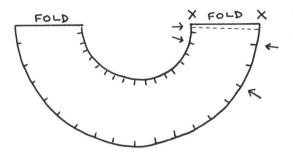

FOLD   X FOLD X

Fig. 77

4. Cut out inner circle: it now resembles a giant 'Polo' mint as in Fig. 76. Fold the fabric exactly on the first two lines (ones with the cross) i.e. the marks lie on the crease. Sew a ½" tuck (Fig. 77). If using metric seam allowances sew .6cm not .5cm on this occasion.

Remember that a tuck is a parallel line <u>not</u> a diagonal one.

Sew tucks on all the marks - 36 tucks in total. Alternate the direction of the stitching to prevent distortion. Use a thread saver (see page 14 of **'Tucks Textures & Pleats'**).

Watch the seam allowance - do not drift in or out at the end of the lines. Take care to align the correct degree marks; check that you are still stitching directly opposing marks.

5. When all the tucks are stitched, press really well turning all the tucks in the same direction. Hopefully it will lie flat!

Should you inadvertently have a 'lampshade' not a flat circle, there is a sneaky way to overcome the problem. By hand, sew just inside the centre hole; use double thread; draw up the centre until it lies flat (Fig. 78). This may cause some bunching but - fret ye not - once the middle has been applied then any little idiosyncrasies and mishaps will be concealed. Have faith!

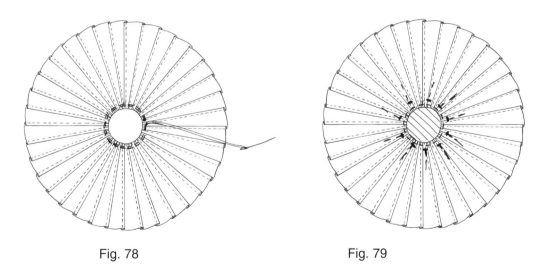

Fig. 78   Fig. 79

6. Place a piece of spare material under the central hole. Pin in place and sew round through all the layers to secure all the tucks (Fig. 79). Do not worry if the hole is not circular: the next stage will improve its appearance.

7. Measure the full diameter of the central space from stitching to stitching. Set the compass for half this measurement and draw a circle on some paper; cut out. This paper circle will be the template for the centre section. Why not experiment with various sized circles and decide which size looks best optically? Position the paper circle in the centre; lightly draw round with a sharp pencil. Stitch round on this line. (Fig. 80). The centre can be hand applied now or later (see stage 9).

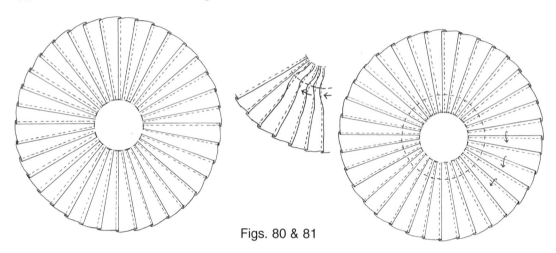

Figs. 80 & 81

8. (At this point the work could be mounted on some wadding/batting to create a quilted effect; do remember to pin the layers well together.) Twist the tucks to create the textured effect. Measure the selected spacing from the corrected circular centre; use a ruler; mark with light pencil dots as in Fig. 81 - these dots will be concealed when the tucks are twisted. Sew round on these marks turning the tucks in the reverse direction (twisting) as you go. Measure again for the next ring of stitches; take the measurements from the corrected centre at all times. This will ensure that all the rows will remain truly circular. This method although the most accurate can be time-consuming. Achieve the same effect with the Quilting Guide. This 'L' shaped piece slots, clips or screws on to some part of the presser foot. Many machines have this small part in the box of attachments but it is not expensive to buy if you do not possess one.

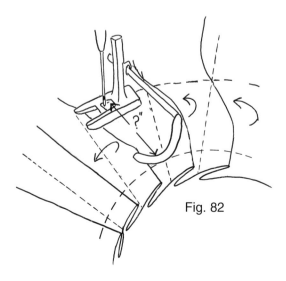

Set the desired measurement between the edge of the guide and the machine needle. The trick is to follow the corrected centre with the tip of the lever thus sewing an exact copy of the circle but x"(xcm) larger (Fig. 82). This is considerably speedier but you have to sew in an anti-clockwise direction rather than the usual clock-wise; in addition accuracy is paramount as you can only follow the previously stitched circle not the original one. Continue with either method until the circle is tucked up.

Fig. 82

9. Complete the centre by cutting a circle of fabric approximately ½"(1.5cm) larger than the paper centre. Tack/baste the fabric to the paper. Attach to the centre with small hand hem/slip stitching; unpick the tacking/basting; turn over and slit the spare piece of fabric; remove the paper through the gap (if desired all this original fabric can be removed).

Using and Experimenting with the Tucked-up Circle

1. Apply the circle to a larger piece of material; pin well and turn the raw edge under; stitch by hand or try the blind hem stitch (see page 75).

a. Use it for the centre of a quilt/wall-hanging or giant floor cushion.

b. Quilt on to wadding/batting with 'tramlines' (parallel lines of stitchery) or some alternative form of decorative stitch. Lash or glue to a board for a textured hanging.

c. Make a small quilt by sandwiching wadding/batting between the circle and some backing material. Quilt the layer together; bind in the usual way.

2. Explore the effect of different centres. Try filling the central hole with ruched fabric (see page 29 of **'Tucks Textures & Pleats'**). Embellish the centre with free machine quilting (page 13). Apply a further textural decoration - the centre can be as creative as you wish.

3. Change the original size of the circle; make it smaller or larger.

4. Sew darts and have a lampshade!

5. Experiment with different quantities of tucks. The tucks can be spaced at any degree marking provided that it divides evenly into 360°. Using less tucks will require a decrease in the diameter of the central hole; vice versa with more tucks.

The size of the central hole is directly determined by the quantity and seam widths of the tucks, viz;

Measuring at 12° will form 30 tucks. 30 tucks x ½"(1.25cm) seam will take 30"(75cm) of material from circumference (remember the tuck is always double the seam as there are two sides). In addition you will require 30 x ½"(30 x 1.25cm) = 15"(37.5cm) extra space for the tucks to lie flat. Therefore the circumference has to be 45"(112.5cm) in total. Dear old Pythagoras now leaps into the equation as you must divide this measurement by 2 x 3.14 to find the new *radius* of the circle.

$$45'' \div (2 \times 3.14) = \textbf{7.2''} \text{ or } 107.5\text{cm} \div (2 \times 3.14) = \textbf{18 cm}$$

All you do is set the compass for this measurement and draw a new inner circle. Suspect this will all sound far too complicated for many of you. It is almost as easy to cut the inner hole larger when you realise that it is not big enough, and tidy up the appearance with the appliqued paper circle. Don't fuss too much, do not forget -

**You can't go wrong.
It is just a little different!**

Now really get confused. Alternate the sizes of the tuck seams - every other one larger or smaller - but you must be consistent or the result will not lie flat.

6. Experiment with pressing the tucks flat as in the 'Crossing Over the Tucks' technique (page 43).

7. Explore the appearance of spiralled lines radiating out from the centre. This requires a little bit of artistic licence as it does not quite 'work' totally evenly. Try it and see!

Fibonacci

Who, what or where is Fibonacci (pronounced Fibbonarchy)? Well, he was a thirteenth century Italian mathematician who developed an arithmetical number series. There are many different number series but this one has some particular attributes and can be utilised to create harmoniously proportioned designs. Having hunted about for some interesting information on this fellow, I was totally stuck but a student of mine, Maureen Mansell-Ward, came up with the goods. Read on for .....

The Tale of Fibonacci

In 1170 somewhere in Pisa Mr and Mrs Fibonacci had a son whom they called Leonardo. He was a bright little child with an amazing mathematical brain, and to his mother's horror he had an over-whelming fetish with rabbits. They moved to North Africa because his father became the consul, and little Leonardo was packed off to school with all the other children. To his delight there was an Arabian Mathematics Master who taught Leonardo all the aspects of calculation, from his tables to long division and other such complicated conundrums. One imagines that the rabbits were very useful as they had reproduced by this time, and when Leonardo ran out of fingers he could always use rabbits to help with the counting; after all rabbits can certainly multiply.

After he left school he decided to become a Mathematician (some people like sums!) By this time he had made so many fascinating discoveries about numbers and their relationship that he decided to write a book. 'Liber abaci' or the 'Book of the Abacus' was published in 1202. Remember that there were no computers in those days merely abacuses, or in Fibonacci's case, rabbits. Through this worthy tome the Arabian number system was brought to Europe.

What did this book reveal? Well, it produced amongst other things a sequence of numbers that resulted from the answer to a recreational problem.

"How many pairs of rabbits can be produced from a single pair in one year if it is assumed that every month each pair begets a new pair which from the second month becomes productive"

Month:	1	2	3	4	5	6	7	8	9	10	11	12	13
No. of pairs:	1	1	2	3	5	8	13	21	34	55	89	144	233

The lower line being the important number series, the next figure in the sequence is always the sum of the previous two e.g. 89 + 144 = 233 rabbits! I imagine that Leonardo's wife was none too pleased at being inundated with bunnies as I am certain she had to clean the hutches and scavenge for tons of dandelion leaves. History does not confirm this supposition.

Time passed and our genius went on to write more books 'Practica geometriae' and 'Liber quadratorum', the latter being a non-fiction best-seller on square numbers. He eventually died sometime after 1240, one would suspect from a surfeit of rabbit stew.

Years later his work was extensively studied by another Italian, Lucas Pacioli, who discovered that the number series also related to the 'Golden Section'. This was an important concept in both ancient and modern artistic and architectural design. It's all tied up with Golden Means, Ratios and Golden Rectangles. I will not bore you with all the tedious details, but suffice it to say that a rectangle whose sides are in the proportions of ⅗ or ⅝ is presumed to be most optically pleasing. Today's modern computers reveal that Fibonacci and the Golden Mean are not quite exact at all times, but near enough to aid in the construction of harmonious space.

With further explorations into his work it was discovered that a spiral can be constructed across an arrangement of squares using the Fibonacci proportions, which is almost the same as the spiral on every mollusc and snail shell in the world. His number sequence is also displayed by the botanical phenomenon known as phyllotaxis (for us lesser mortals this is the arrangement of leaves and petals on a stem). Thus the whorls on a pinecone or pineapple, petals on a sunflower and branches on some stems follow the Fibonacci spiral.

In fact we are all living examples of this number system. Take the first set of figures in the series 1,2,3,5, (frequently the first 1 is ignored) and see it as multiplication of a 'unit' – the unit can be any specified measurement. Now look at your hands: no matter how big the first little bone in your finger is, the second bone is 2 x the first one, the third bone is 3 x and the fourth one (looking at the back of the hand) is 5 x the first. In very simple terms and selecting a totally haphazard measurement assume the first bone measures 1"(2.5cm); then the second is 2"(5cm), third 3"(7.5cm) and the fourth 5"(12.5cm), and the result is exceedingly big hands! The same phenomenon occurs in your feet. We are used to seeing these proportions and they appear to be totally normal and thoroughly acceptable to the human eye.

How on earth does one use the system? It can be employed in many layouts to create a harmonious proportion between the shapes, spaces and areas; such as in the pieces for Strip Patchwork, Log Cabin, Seminole or any other form of design that takes strips of material, by cutting out all the strips in Fibonacci related measurements e.g. 1"(2.5cm), 2"(5cm), 3"(7.5cm) etc. When stuck for an idea for bordering a quilt/wall-hanging, experiment with adding extra frames cut out in Fibonacci proportioned widths rather than having all the same width. If you are working in a rectangular shape, by making the sides in the ⅗ or ⅝ ratio or even ⅝₃ the overall effect will be visually pleasing and naturally balanced.

Using Fibonacci in Strips

The sequence is : 1,2,3,5,8,13, 21 - next digit in the series is always the sum of the previous two.

You select the unit of measurement i.e. 1"(2.5cm); this is then multiplied by the sequence. Thus you will have a strip of 1"(2.5cm), 2"(5cm), 3"(7.5cm), 5"(10cm) ad infinitum. It must be appreciated that an 1"(2.5cm) rapidly becomes very large, so you may prefer to select a smaller unit of measurement.

Do not forget that the unit of measurement must always be the same.

Having decided on the unit of measurement cut out some strips, *remembering to add on the seam allowance before you cut out*. These strips can now be formed into a band. Watch that you alternate the direction of the stitching (Fig. 83). The seams may be ironed open or closed whichever is preferable. Pressing the seams closed is speedier but causes a small ridge on one side of the seam due to two layers of material. Pressing the seams open makes the strip appear flatter as the seams are evenly divided.

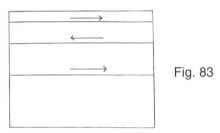

Fig. 83

Deliberately I have not mentioned colour with regard to Fibonacci; but take care when selecting colours as the differing widths of the strips may not look quite so pleasing if the colour balance is up the creek! It may be preferable to work with an analogous scheme (colours side by side on the Colour Wheel - see Glossary) rather than a complimentary one (colours directly opposite on the Colour Wheel).

The stitched strip can now be cut up in a variety of ways.

1. Squares can be turned into various designs such as 'Rail and Fence' or pin-wheeled round to form a block.

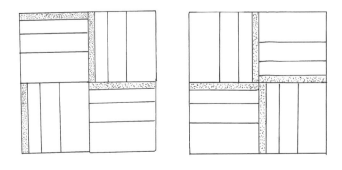

2. Cut 45° or 60° triangles and link in a variety of ways.

3. Experiment with 'Seminole' designs cut from the band

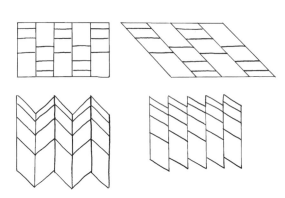

4. There are many different ways of using Fibonacci within any strip system. One interesting way of utilising the strip is shown in Fig. 84. *Sadly there is a snag to this design - the first strip gets obliterated in the diagonal seam.*

It's well worth making a further band increasing the size of the first strip in the series by approx ½"(1.25cm); then the colour will still show after the triangles have been pieced together.

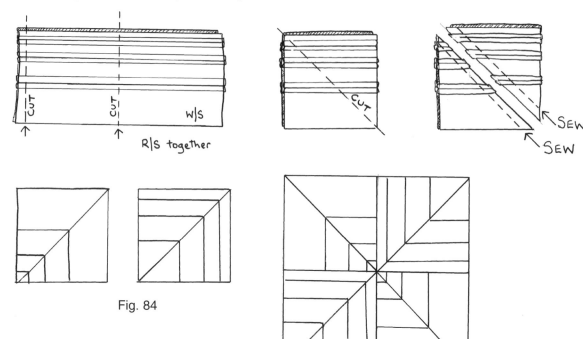

Fig. 84

Cut the strip in half; place R/S together (matching colours and strips); cut into squares. ***Keep the squares R/S together*** and divide on the diagonal forming pairs of triangles *(do not split the pairs)*. Stitch the down the diagonals, matching up the seams. Open out the squares and form into the design as in Fig. 84.

5. What about a 'Trip round the World' constructed from a Fibonacci cylinder?

Or a 'Bargello' style of design? There are a variety of books on the 'cylinder system' which is an easy method of rotating colours to produce exciting designs.

Photograph of a miniature 'Trip Round the World' (10″ x 12″).

The nicest thing about designs using the Fibonacci sequence is that not many of the seams match up as the strips are all different sizes.

Using Fibonacci in Squares

Squares can be linked together to form a rectangle and it is the curve across this rectangle that is the naturally occurring spiral (Fig. 85). In this instance the first 1 in the series is re-introduced. The curve can be formed by inserting the compass point in one corner of the square, stretch to the opposite diagonal corner and draw the arc.

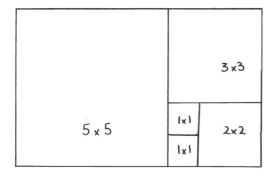

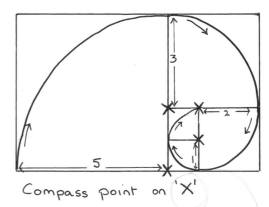

Compass point on 'X'

Fig. 85

Why not try making up Log Cabin blocks in the relevant sizes and linking together for a very different creative design; or what about using Interlocking Squares for a textured effect?

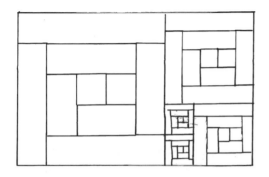 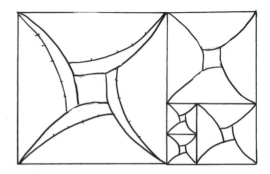

Explore the use of colour in this design of Fibonacci related squares and rectangles. This cannot be done with any strip method – *all the pieces have to cut individually.*

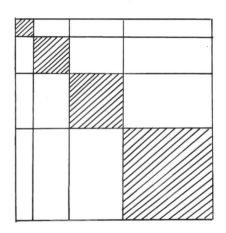

Play with the square sizes to construct original patterns, overlapping in Fibonacci proportions, or experiment with other shapes such as triangles (cut squares in half on the diagonal) for a fascinating layout. Several Quilt designers have used the number series to create interesting hangings working with hexagons, rectangles and spirals. It can be done but may require a little artistic licence.

Tuck a square of fabric with tucks at Fibonacci related spacings. Twist the tucks as they cross. Embellish with machine quilting. See coloured photograph.

Trace off the Fibonacci Spiral and use it for designing. Flip the spiral over, interlink, repeat, expand, contract and even distort. Interpret the resulting creation in Bias Strips or maybe as a Quilting Pattern.

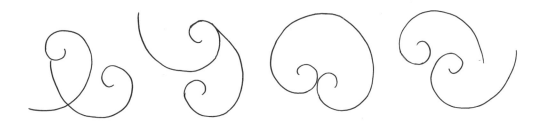

Why was Fibonacci included in this book? He has nothing to do with texture but his number system has all sorts of uses, and those with slightly jaded palettes, bored with the usual sets of geometric shapes, may like to explore a new avenue; who knows what will happen then?

A final thought: was it the burrowing of all the rabbits he kept that was responsible for the leaning Tower of Pisa?

Fibonacci related spirals (Chris Day)

Dyeing
in the
Microwave

I have firmly resisted the temptation to call this chapter 'Have Fun Dying in the Microwave', or even 'Dying to have Fun in the Microwave', as this fascinating method of creating colour is far from a grave procedure. The last thing I would like to do is to dissuade anyone from trying to dye.

This is real fun, exceptionally quick, very easy and can be most economical. Dip the cloth in the dye solution, rinse and dry – what could be simpler than that! All sorts of patterns, colours and creative effects can be speedily achieved from plain tints, tones and shades to fabulous dyed and over-dyed designs in only a few minutes. Any type of microwave may be used and there is no need for specialized equipment other than ordinary household items like old yoghurt pots and clingfilm. The dye is readily available from most hardware, art and craft shops or sometimes department stores, and you can mix up your own colours from the dyes to create many more exciting and original hues. The dyed material will have a fabulous mottled appearance and although you can get a fairly even colour, the whole appeal of this type of dying is the variegated finish. If you really want the colour to be evenly spread, then I do suggest that you go out and buy pre-dyed fabric.

The one drawback to this technique is that you can only use natural fibres and the cloth must be well washed first. So what better use for all those old cotton sheets that languish at the back of the cupboard (does anyone turn sides to middle these days?), and as an extra bonus they are already well washed.

The best thing about this technique is :-

You can't go really wrong!

The resulting colour may not be quite what you intended but does it matter? Dye another bit; it only takes a minute or two and then you will have two pieces and you can choose which is the better. Should you over-cook the fabric, it will get a little crisp and if you under-cook, the colour will be paler in shade and a lot of dye will come out in the rinsing. In this case, cook for a few seconds longer next time.

Textured Landscape (14" x 11") with basket of microwave dyed fabrics and circular 'Trip round World' (30") also constructed from dyed material (Jennie Rayment).

Padded Sculptured Sphere (11") with microwave dyed calico (Jennie Rayment).

Round Fabric Basket, Interlocking Squares and Corners on Log Cabin (Jennie Rayment).

'Canadian Rockies' (47″ x 32″) - hanging constructed with Interlocking Squares (Val Morgan).

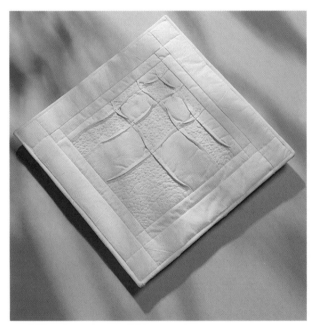

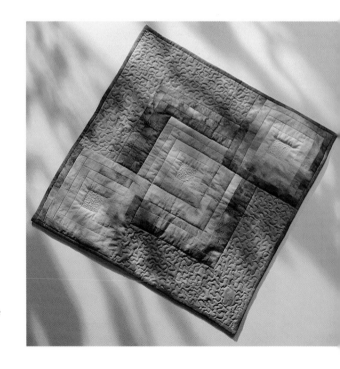

Fibonacci series spaced tucks in calico (Jennie Rayment).

Quilt (41″ square) designed from Fibonacci related areas in microwave dyed shades; machine quilted (Jennie Rayment)

Health and Safety

ALL DYE POWDERS ARE HARMFUL AND MUST BE TREATED WITH CARE

DO NOT inhale or ingest the powder – this applies to all dye powders not especially dyes suited to the microwave. Wear rubber gloves, and if this is the first time you have ever used any dye, it is a good idea to wear a paper face mask as one in a million people can suffer a curious reaction to the dye powder; but if you have used dyes before you should be perfectly all right. The microwave is safe to use for dyeing provided you keep everything well sealed and covered when cooking. Ensure that all items used for dyeing are not used again for normal cooking purposes unless they are exceptionally well washed. How to clean the microwave is described on page 69.

Now, having thoroughly put you off the whole process just let me add that I have dyed vast quantities of fabric and have suffered no ill effects other than my usual battiness and normal inability to spell.

Which Dye to Buy?

In my opinion Dylon Hand Dye for Natural Fabrics works better than any other dye that I have yet discovered. You can purchase a wide range of colours, but from red, blue, yellow, green and black an enormous range of tints, tones and shades may be achieved. There are various different sorts of dye manufactured by Dylon and the one that you require comes in a small box, not the round tin; but do check with the store if you are not sure.

So collect up the fabric, do put on old clothes and wear rubber gloves.

Going out to supper or greeting the family with multi-coloured hands does not look very appealing. It takes several days for the skin to assume its normal tones.

Preparing the Material

Rip your fabric into approx 18" (46cm) squares. (Cloth is best used dry, damp fabric makes the concentration of dye colour weaker.) For intriguing and interesting special dyed effects, the fabric needs to be prepared; try pleating either straight across or on the diagonal (pleats will retain the pattern better if you press them). Lashing with string in different places or knotting produces fascinating designs – lash or knot firmly to prevent the dye seeping into the cloth.

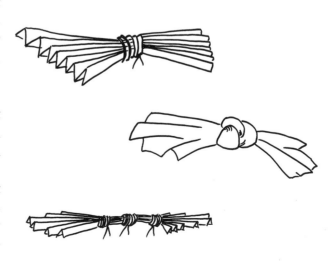

Remember that the more you lash the fabric the less it will absorb the dye and you will have areas of white material. Why not scrunch the material into a tight ball before wrapping firmly with string?

Try folding the fabric into a concertina - either as a square or perhaps as a triangle - then lash it with string in various places. This can be dyed in one corner then overdyed in the other corners to create bizarre effects.

 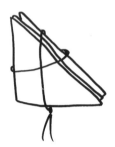

What about tying things into parts of the material? Corks are very effective when tied in relevant places; experiment with pattern or just tie them in anywhere and appreciate the abstract result. Buttons could be used to create a further design. In fact you can tie all sorts of objects into the cloth, but *do remember they must be non-metallic.*

I have tried many assorted household items to see if they would produce an amazingly different pattern, and realized that not all objects come out the same shape as they began; for instance the plastic tart cutter will never make round tarts again. So a word of caution: just check that the desired object will withstand the heat of the microwave!

An unusual design can be created by painting a selection of dye colours on to the individually tied corks or buttons. Slosh the dye on with an old household paintbrush; the colours will bleed into each other and resemble those wonderful colour studies of Impressionist painters. For a more defined appearance, cook the fabric after painting some of the corks, then paint others and cook again. Remember you can always overdye. It does not appear to matter how many times you cook the fabric.

Preparing the Dye Solution

The instruction on the packet (usually written in very small print) will state how to use the entire box of dye. It is much better to use the dye pro rata i.e.

1 heaped teaspoon (approx. 10gm) of dye powder
dissolved in 2 fluid ozs (60cc) of tepid water.

(This makes it very economical when dyeing small pieces as only a small quantity of dye solution is necessary. The dyes are strong and being overgenerous with the dye powder can result in harsh colours.)

Put the dye powder into a yoghurt pot or beaker and carefully add the water, stirring well to dissolve it using an old teaspoon or throwaway plastic one (the quantity of disposable spoons is one of the best things about airline meals). Tepid water helps the dye to dissolve faster.

Mixing colours

To make different colours – mix dry powders first before adding the water.

Red + Blue = Purple
Red + Yellow = Orange
Yellow + Blue = Green
Black + Red + Yellow = Brown
Red + Green = Brown

Mixing the dye powders creates superb effects. Shades of orange come from red and yellow mixed; make browns by adding a very small quantity of black to red and yellow – various tones are made by different proportions of the colours. Varying hues of green can be produced by either mixing blue and yellow – considerably more yellow than blue (yellow dye seems to be weaker in concentration than the other colours and you always need more than you think) – or change the green dye powder by adding more yellow, blue and possibly a little black. Go easy on the black, a little goes a long way so do go very sparingly with it. Purples are created from red and blue mixed in different quantities.

If you are likely to want more of any colour it is well worth jotting down a few notes on quantities and proportions of dye powder.

(A small word of advice: be very specific with your notes and be aware that to get the identical colour is almost impossible because there are too many variables and you would need to have exactly the same set of circumstances. Look at Nature's imperfections – is anything quite the same?)

Dyeing the Fabric

The best receptacles to cook the dyed cloth in are ½ gall/½ ltr ice-cream or coleslaw type containers. These are readily available from supermarket delicatessen counters either free or for a small charge. If you are unable to obtain this sort of plastic box then an old Tupperware or similar kind of container would be suitable. Failing to get any of the latter then a microwaveable dish with a well-fitting lid will suffice. For extra safety place the box into a microwaveable polythene bag or cover the lid with a layer of clingfilm.

Put the prepared fabric into the dye and work solution well into the cloth. *WEAR RUBBER GLOVES*; failing to do so means strangely coloured hands for days! Squeeze out excess dye and place the cloth into the plastic or microwaveable container; seal well before cooking on *HIGH* for 1min 30sec - 1min 50sec. Most microwaves are 600 – 750 watts so if yours is a different wattage, simply adjust the times a little. If you overcook the material it will be somewhat crisp; if you have undercooked the cloth the dye will not take so well.

To obtain a more evenly coloured surface, tip the dye solution and fabric into a tough polythene bag and rub the dye into the cloth.

Carefully remove the container from the microwave and allow to cool before removing the lid. Take the dyed sample out with tongs; let the fabric cool before removing any knots or string etc; this helps to set the dye.

Rinse it well in cold water until the colour ceases to flood out; wash in warm soapy water; rinse again in cold water before drying and using.

Remember to wash the container well before adding the next piece of material
as you can get contamination of the new piece by the old colour.

(Don't do as I have done and cheat on the washing and rinsing and throw it all in the machine with other things - unless you wish to have even more multi-coloured washing than usual.)

Easy isn't it!

Making Tints of the Same Colour

Technically a tint is a colour to which white has been added to produce a lighter hue. Make tints by mixing in white or by diluting the original solution. You can create several different tints in descending order of paleness by mixing a larger amount of dye solution to begin with i.e. 2 heaped teaspoonfuls + 4 fluid ozs (120cc) water. Divide the solution into two pots, approx. 2 fl oz (60cc) in each pot; keep one pot untouched, add 2 fl oz (60cc) to the other, stir well then divide again into two; keep one pot aside and add 2 fl oz (60cc) water to the other, stir and divide again. This can be done several times producing 5 - 6 different shades from one hue (Fig. 86).

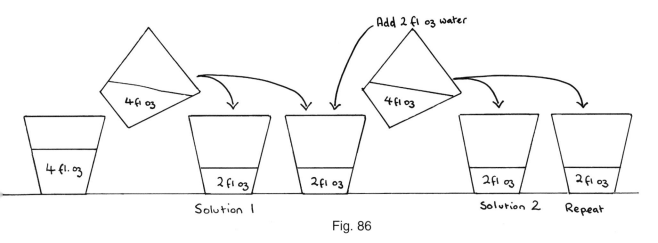

Fig. 86

Special Effects

Microwaved dyeing creates an interesting mottled design on the surface, but you can further enhance the effect in a variety of ways.

1. Fold the fabric into squares, tie with string to keep it in place before dipping one corner only into the dye solution, cook, then re-dip the other corner into another colour, cook again. If the effect is not pleasing when you have cooled the cloth then over-dye with another colour. It is possible to fold the cloth in many different ways, cooking several times to dye all or part of it.

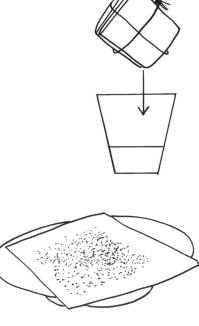

2. Lay a damp cloth on an old plate, lightly sprinkle with dry dye powder. Flick droplets of water on to the dye. This causes the colours to bleed making an intriguing stippled surface. Try several different colours at the same time.

3. Wrap fabric round an old wooden rolling pin, lash with string, then paint with different dye colours. (Old household paintbrushes are ideal.) This results in a striped fabric and totally depends whether you rolled the fabric diagonally or straight on to the pin. It is possible to drape the fabric over the end of the pin, then lash in place. (Tie a button in the centre before you drape.) Very thick short lengths of drainpipe will work as well. Increase the time of the cooking to allow for the extra density of the pin or drainpiping.

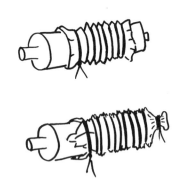

4. Lay the cloth in the microwaveable container and spoon different colours on to it to create a space-dyed effect. Experiment with damp or dry cloth; the dye will bleed more on damp fabric.

5. Tie corks or old buttons (*plastic or wood only*) into the fabric. Try painting each lump a different colour; if you paint all the bits at once the colours will bleed into each other. Try cooking a section at a time.

6. Experiment with other natural fabrics, perhaps linen or silk. Cotton/polyester mixtures do dye but the colour is weak. *DO NOT USE VISCOSE OR RAYON* as these may give off harmful fumes. Silk takes moments to dye, so reduce the time a little.

7. See the difference between damp and dry fabrics dipped into the same pot. Put two small pieces in at the same time and the damper one will absorb less dye and naturally come out a different tint.

Finally use up all the dye solutions either by mixing together, which usually produces a good 'yucky' brown shade, or by tipping the bits left on to some cloth placed in the container. One of the nicest pieces that I made came from wiping the work-surface and some spilt dye and then cooking it!

Dyeing Larger or Smaller Quantities of Material

Dyeing larger pieces is just as easy; simply make more dye solution and increase the time for cooking. I suggest that ½ yard/metre will take approximately two minutes and will need 3 heaped spoonfuls of dye dissolved in six fluid ounces of tepid water. 1½ yards/metres will take approximately four minutes at full power and will need almost the entire packet of dye. Unless you have a very large microwave and container, the dye diffusion is a little blotchy and you are better advised to dye large pieces in the washing machine, using the special dye for machines.

Small quantities are the reverse: shorten the cooking time, but it is not so easy to reduce the dye quantity unless you have very accurate measuring equipment at home, although you can always dye a further piece in the remaining solution. The second dyeing from the same dilution will always be a little lighter than the first.

Cleaning the Microwave

After use, wash the inside really well with warm soapy water. Peel a potato, slice thinly, cook on a piece of kitchen roll, then throw the potato away. There is just a chance that some dye molecules may have escaped all the careful covering of the containers; so to prevent the highly unlikely chance of them getting into your food, the cooking of raw sliced potatoes will absorb anything floating around.

So roll up your sleeves, don the apron,
clear out the lodger from the kitchen and get dyeing.
Why not dye fabrics to make a Textured Landscape ?
Dye the cloth for that fabulous embroidery?
Just take a little care with the safety side,
then you too will live to read the next page.

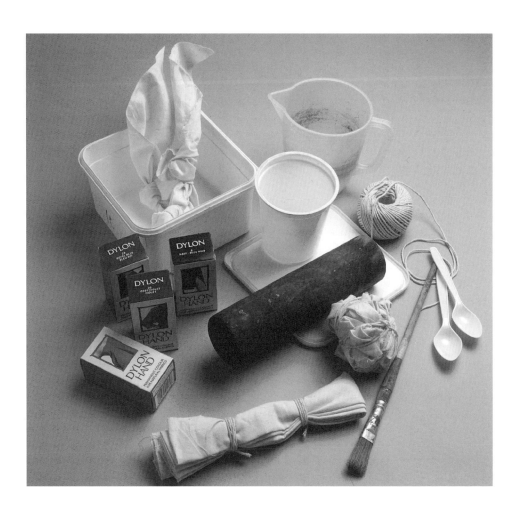

Textured

Landscapes

Collect together an array of landscape coloured fabrics, search out a photograph or a postcard or even a cutting from a magazine, and launch into your own creative textured panorama. There is no reason why you have to copy an existing photograph; use your own imagination and draw your own scene - at least no one can say that it does not resemble the original.

The best pictures have easily defined areas of fields, hills, mountains and sky with lots of interesting colours and textures. Scenes with craggy rocks, old stone walls, hedgerows and possibly a lake or two will give you plenty of scope to work with. Artistic licence is permitted and a little bit of deviation from the specified model never hurt anyone and are they ever going to know? If Salvador Dali can have drooping clocks all over his pictures, a minor misalignment of the hills is never going to be noticed. Take heart and ignore anything in the least bit complicated and simplify the chosen picture. If you are creating from your imagination, plug into naive mode; after all simplicity is often the best policy.

Many of the textured ideas that can be modified for landscapes are expanded in **'Tucks Textures & Pleats'** but the essence is contained in this chapter. So find an intriguing vista or charge up your imagination and create an original.

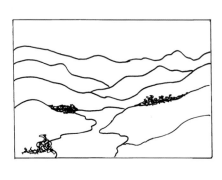

landscape

portrait

Decide on the size of your landscape. It can be any size from a large wall-hanging to a small picture. If this is the first attempt, a good average size could be 24"(60cm) x 18"(45cm) - either a landscape or portrait type of picture.

Preparation

Begin by cutting a piece of lightweight sew-in vilene a little larger than the chosen landscape size. Roughly sketch the main lines of the picture. Then cut some 2oz wadding/batting slightly bigger than the vilene.

Pin these layers together. It is unnecessary to place any fabric on the back of the two layers; most machines will cope with the wadding. Should you find that the wadding catches on the feed-dogs, placing some paper underneath can prevent the problem (any thin paper will suffice - no need to use `Stitch and Tear'). The paper tears off easily afterwards.

Using a base of wadding/batting and lightweight sew-in vilene helps considerably in the construction of the landscape .

Method

The landscape is constructed using the 'Quilt-as-you-go' technique, sometimes referred to as 'Stitch and Flip'. With this method the pieces are stitched together through the wadding thus creating an instant quilted effect. The use of the vilene prevents the wadding from stretching and distorting in addition to providing a surface to draw on.

1. Begin at the top of the picture with the sky fabrics or the top part of the desired creation. Cut the first strip the width of the landscape, and place R/S up at the top. Pin in place and stitch the edge to secure (Fig. 87). *Remember that you are stitching through all the layers.*

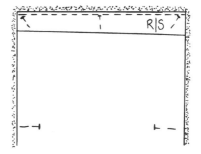

2. Cut more strips of varying colours, lengths and widths. Place the next strip R/S down on to the previous one, stitch the lower edge (Fig. 88). Fold (flip) back, finger press firmly and pin down (this ensures that the strip will not move or distort - most important if you are making a large piece of work).

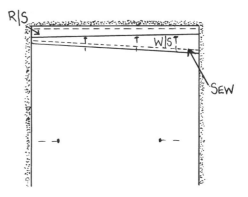

Figs. 87 & 88

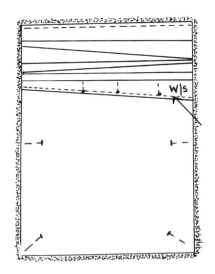

Continue adding the pieces in this manner until you have completed the top/sky section. Experiment with the positioning of the strips as these can be angled to produce the streaks that are found in cloud formations. Trim any excess material from the seams or the remnants of the under strip may show through.

Creating the Textured Sections

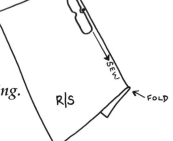

Allow extra material when texturing.

1. Rock Formations

With the zipper foot on the machine small tucks made be made that resemble crags and cracks in geological strata. Select the correct colour of fabric; fold the material and placing the edge of the zipper foot on the fold of the cloth, sew down the edge (Fig. 89).

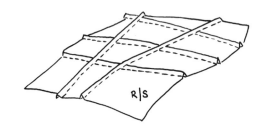

Fig. 89

This will produce a narrow tuck similar to a pin tuck. Experiment with tucks in all directions thus constructing the rocky appearance of mountains.

2. Ruched 'Forests'

Scrunched or ruched material conjures up the illusion of forests and trees, or if really gathered tightly could be more geological formation. Ruching 'eats' fabric; start with a piece approximately 4 x larger than required. Thread the machine with toning thread, top and bottom bobbin. Tighten top thread tension (aids the gathering process - unless the machine gathers the fabric instantly on sewing in which case return the top tension to normal).

Set stitch at maximum length.

Keeping the rows of stitch ¾"(2cm) apart, sew from side to side sewing across the fabric, jumping to the next row and sewing back (Fig. 90).

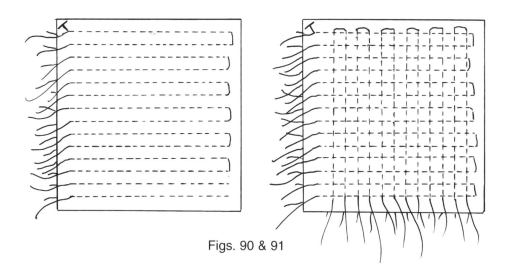

Figs. 90 & 91

Leave the thread ends for pulling up. Repeat the stitching pattern from the top to the bottom (Fig. 91). Pull all the ends up until the cloth is gathered sufficiently for the desired effect. As a precaution mark the top side of the material with a T and watch that you only pull the threads on this side; accidentally pulling the threads on the underside will cause the threads to lock. Be systematic in the thread pulling - pull up all pairs of threads on one edge first, then do the other edge.

Closely spaced lines of stitch = scrunch.
Widely spaced lines of stitch = lumps!

Construct stone walls or hedgerows by gathering a strip along both sides and then pulling the threads up. (Remember to keep the stitch length at maximum when gathering.) This band can be manipulated into various different shapes. Attach by placing R/S down, stitch the edge, fold back and re-pin or stitch the outer edge to secure (Fig. 92).

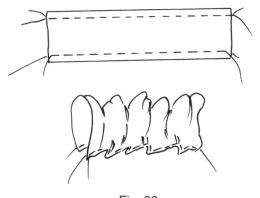

Fig. 92

3.'Folds in the Hills'

Experiment with folds in the material to resemble the undulations of valleys and fields. Fold the fabric at different angles to create a scenic effect. Pin well in place, or secure the folds by stitching in between then re-folding to hide the stitching (Fig. 93).

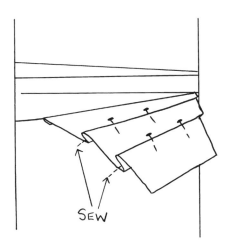

SEW

Fig. 93

4. 'Ploughed Fields'

Construct a panel of tucks to give an impression of furrows or ridges in a field, possibly for a roof or some form of slats in fencing. Cut a strip of fabric the length of the textured area and at least 2 - 3 x desired width. Along the width (longer side) make small marks 1"(2.5cm) apart (Fig. 94). (The 1"(2cm) measurement is arbitrary - make marks at any spacing to suit the objective.)

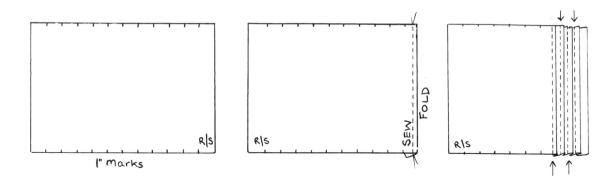

Fig. 94

Fold the fabric on the marks; using ¼"(.5cm) seam allowance, sew down the fold. This will create a tuck (Fig. 94). Continue until the piece is the desired width and press all the tucks in one direction. Alternate the direction when sewing the tucks; try to sew from one edge to the other to prevent any distortion of the fabric.

See 'Tucks Textures & Pleats' (page 14) for the thread saver tip and further ideas with tucks.

5. Grasses and 'Faraway Forests'!

Rip material and fringe the edge to create the soft fronds of grass or the misty contours of far distant woodlands. The torn material frays best; tear off a piece the length and width that you require, place R/S up, pin and stitch along the edge (Fig. 95). (Keep the stitching line as close to the outer edge as possible then the seam will be concealed when you attach the next section.) Fray back after inserting, which is considerably easier than attempting to stitch a heavily fringed strip. Tearing a wider strip means that you fold it in half and have double the frayed appearance.

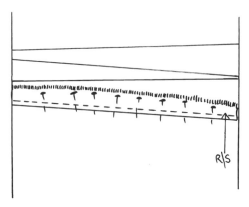

Fig. 95

Adding the Textured Sections to the Landscape

Attach the various pieces as in 'Quilt-as-you-go'. Place the textured segment R/S down, pin in place, then stitch before flipping back, finger pressing and re-pinning down. If this is not possible for some reason apply the section using either a hand stitch or a machine stitch.

By hand: pin in place, roll the raw edges under and secure with either blanket, slip, hem or a feather stitch. What about a decorative embroidery pattern? Embellish the rolled edge with experimental stitchery or attach some braid for further textural creativity!

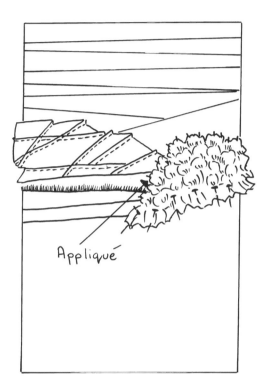

Appliqué

By machine: try out the blind hem stitch. This stitch is extremely useful for machine appliqué. Many sewing machines have this stitch in their repertoire but not all of them can balance the stitch length and width to create the best effect.

Use the normal straight stitch presser foot or the open embroidery one:
stitch length 1 : stitch width 1
This changes the stitch appearance and renders it nearly invisible. Try to keep the straight stitching on the outside of the appliqué; the indentation alone holds the material in place. (These settings may have to be modified for some of the latest machines.)

If the inevitable happens and there is a little gap or it proves very difficult to stitch a raw edge down, appliqué another piece on top. No one will ever know that small smidgeon stuck on top is not part of the intended masterpiece!

Completing the Creation

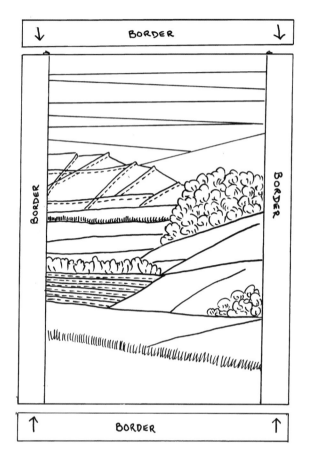

BORDER

BORDER

BORDER

BORDER

Fig. 96

Trim all the edges level: rule one line along a side and draw another one parallel to this on the opposite side; on the remaining sides draw two further lines parallel to each other and at right angles to the first set. Stitch round fractionally inside the line to secure all the pieces then cut any excess away. Add borders by stitching strips to the sides; fold back and stitch further strips to the top and bottom (Fig. 96). Once the borders have been completed, the landscape could be backed, bound and hung from a sleeve or tabs; or you could take the easy way out and stick on to a piece of board or thick card and then hang. If you intend the picture to be a cushion, refer to the Finishing Techniques in **'Tucks Textures & Pleats'**.

Cutting each pair of strips at the same length will keep the landscape squared up.
N.B. The pairs will be of differing lengths - measure each set carefully.

To back the landscape: cut some wadding and a piece of suitable material for the back (medium-weight calico is fine) slightly larger than the completed picture; create a textile sandwich of backing material, wadding and the picture; tack the three layers together working from the centre outwards.

Suggest that you anchor the backing material to a table with masking tape or to the floor with pins to prevent any wrinkles in the cloth.

Prior to binding the raw edges, run a tacking stitch along the outer rim to hold the textile sandwich firmly. The binding could be attached in the same manner as the borders, i.e. add strips to opposite sides then add strips to the remaining sides. Fold towards the back of the work, turn the raw edge under and slip/hem stitch in place.

Fig. 97

Adding tabs can be done before you finally slip-stitch the binding in place. Ensure that any tabs are exactly the same length and positioned evenly or the hanging could be crooked. A sleeve is an easier option (Fig. 97). Flat wooden slats inserted into the sleeve will hold the hanging closer to the wall than a round dowel; holes for picture hooks are easily drilled.

Final Finishing Touch

Titivate the foreground with a few three-dimensional flowers or leaves. Make a template as you may wish to repeat the design. Draw a flower or leaf shape on card keeping the outline simple, and if this is your first attempt don't draw anything too small. Cut out for a template.

1. Take two scraps of fabric plus a piece of 4oz wadding slightly larger than the template.

2. Draw round the template on to the top material, sandwich the wadding between the two layers; pin firmly.

3. Stitch round the outline using either a very small stitch with the normal presser foot or use the darning/hopper foot (running the machine quickly and moving the work slowly to make very small stitches). Trim back all the layers extremely close to the stitching.

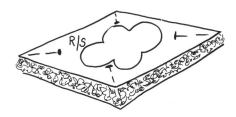

Fig. 98

4. Set the machine for satin stitch (close zig-zag); stitch round three times (Fig. 98). Remember to use the appliqué presser foot (frequently the plastic see-through foot or the one that has an indentation underneath).

1st Round - stitch width 3, stitch length 1: sew round the shape grasping the flower/leaf firmly as you manoeuvre the machine along the edge. The needle goes into the shape and off the edge thus sealing the raw fabric.

2nd Round - stitch width 3.5, stitch length .75: sew round again. The second row will cover the first, building up a firm seal.

3rd Round - stitch width 4, stitch length .5: sew round yet again.

These three rows of stitches will seal the edge and the tightly packed satin stitch causes some distortion thus enhancing the three dimensional effect. Position the flowers and leaves in place and attach by hand stitching.

For the Finale

Hang the landscape, stand back and admire.

Never forget that works of art should always be viewed from a distance to obtain the maximum dynamic imagery.

Now make another one with a different arrangement. How about using heavily textured white materials to conjure up a snow scene? Explore the textural qualities of the sea and introduce nets, chiffons and glittering fabrics for the froth and the foam.

Textured Landscapes (17″ x 19″ & 13½″ x 17″) mounted on boards (Jennie Rayment).

Silk and Calico Contrariwise Cathedral Window (16″) frilled cushion (Jennie Rayment).

Christmas Fabric Baskets (Jennie Rayment)

Textured Scrip Bag using 'Bias Bobble' and twisted tucks in central panel,
Padded Sculptured Sphere (Jennie Rayment) with 15″ Interlocked Hexagon Cushion (Pam Balls).

Bread Basket with Ruched Napkin Ring, tablecloth and circular mat
(Jennie Rayment)

Rectangular Corners on Log Cabin cushion (20″ x 18″) with 3D
Sculptured Spheres (Jennie Rayment)

Bring

on the Bags

As you will have discovered, alliteration is one of my favourite grammatical styles in addition to tautology which is saying the same thing twice e.g. 'added extra'. My dearly beloved proof readers remonstrate frequently with me, and both metaphorically and literally rap my knuckles which can make the typing even more difficult. As I am an awkward 'so and so' or an obstreperous 'whatsit', I shall continue to hack my way through the English language.

So we shall 'Bring on the Bags' and waffle on.

In this chapter you will discover how to make several bags of varying types from a Scrip to the woven handbag (see cover of **'Tucks Textures & Pleats'**) plus a 'sausage' or bolster bag.

All the bags can be increased or decreased in size as required, so you could create multitudinous bags from vast carpet ones to wee diddy ones (tautology again) and, of course, all sizes in between. These may be highly textured or as plain as you like, and why not make simple ones from furnishing materials, corduroys, chintzes or from any material of your choice?

The Scrip Bag

Way back in the olden times, around 1220 - 1270, the Pilgrims toiled their weary way to Canterbury, and on this arduous journey in addition to a back pack, tent and other worldly goods, they carried a small bag - a scrip. It was very difficult to find the essential bits that were immediately necessary on the journey, so the scrip was very useful for holding credit cards, sandwiches and a spare length of knicker elastic. To be serious for a moment, this type of hold-all was only employed at this period of time and is a special design, being more of a balloon shape than a flat pouch.

Now re-designed with extra features, it still maintains the original basic appearance and is ideal for everyone from teenagers to the more mature. The size can be altered. The textural nature of the flap can be modified either plain or as fancy as you wish. One could be made to match that fancy outfit. What is more it makes a lovely hat!

If you should choose to wear the bag as a hat, please remove the contents or you may discover that the sandwiches are a little squashed, and of course the hat won't look very fetching with the contents distorting the overall appearance. Not only can it be worn as a sun shield for the back of the neck, but it is brilliant for calming recalcitrant children as the flap neatly covers the face when worn the other way. I suggest that you make a least half-a-dozen!

To make the basic bag you need:-

20"/½ metre fabric (min 44"/112cm wide) for outside - possibly lightweight furnishing or medium weight cotton material.
20"/½ metre fabric (min 44"/112cm wide) for the lining.
20"/½ metre lightweight iron-on vilene.
20"/½ metre 2oz wadding.
20"/½ metre ½"/12mm elastic.
Button, bead or toggle for fastening.
Matching thread.
[Optional 1" squared paper for drafting].

The bag has an inner pocket and is made from three pieces. **The patterns are shown to scale (the grid relates to inches)** and can either be drawn to the correct size by the grid method, i.e. re-draw the grid in inches and copy the lines in the same spaces, or make life easy by photocopying, enlarging to the desired size. The handle can be adjusted to fit any length.

See next page for patterns

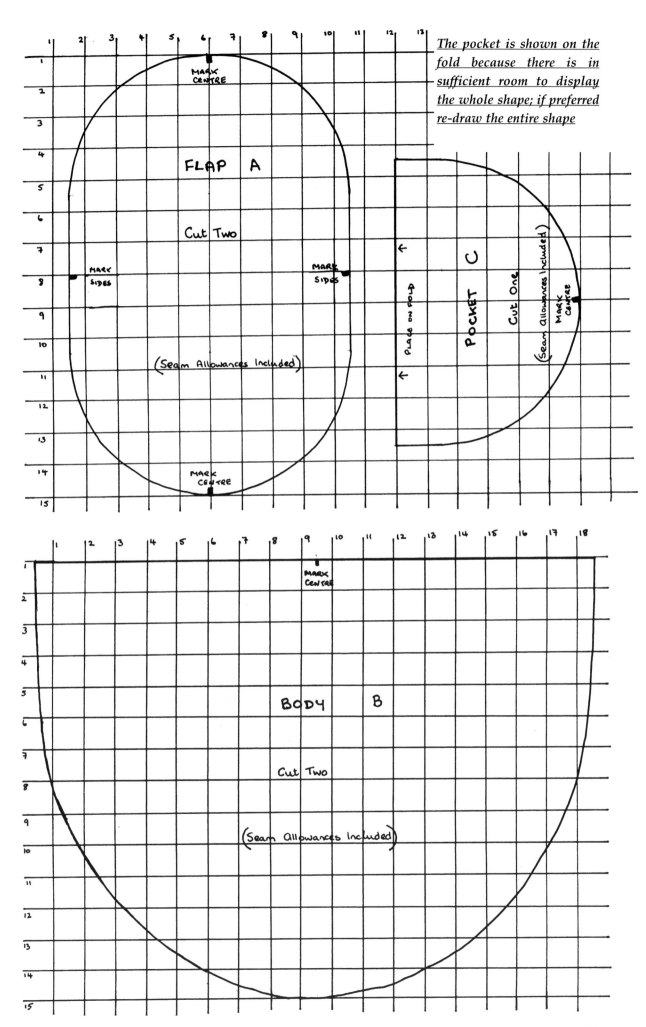

FLAP A

Cut Two

(Seam Allowances Included)

MARK CENTRE

MARK SIDES

MARK SIDES

MARK CENTRE

The pocket is shown on the fold because there is in sufficient room to display the whole shape; if preferred re-draw the entire shape

POCKET C

Cut One

PLACE ON FOLD

(Seam Allowances Included)

MARK CENTRE

BODY B

Cut Two

MARK CENTRE

(Seam Allowances Included)

Making Up

Use a generous ¼"(.75cm) seam allowance; this is not obligatory, but do be consistent!

1. Make templates of the patterns. Pattern pieces A and B are used for the outside of the bag. A, B and C are for the lining.

2. Cut out pattern pieces, check that pocket C is placed on the fold before you cut out. Transfer all matching-up marks to fabric. The outside sections of the bag and the pocket lining need to be reinforced with iron-on vilene (this is not necessary if the fabric is heavyweight such as firm chintz or brocade). *Tip: Cut out shapes in vilene, iron on W/S of fabric before cutting round the pattern.*

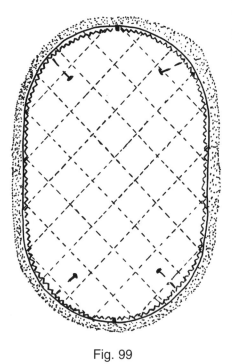

Fig. 99

3. Cut out tab - 1¼"/3cm x 4½"/12cm and strap 4½"/12cm x 44"/112cm approximately (join if necessary). Ensure that the strap is cut across the cloth i.e. from selvedge to selvedge.

4. Place the outer flap section of bag A on to 2oz wadding, and roughly cut out (approx. ½"/1cm) round shape. *Press the material gently to the wadding (ironing helps to hold the fabric to the wadding), pin well.*

5. Quilt the shape to the wadding. The easiest way is to sew diagonal lines across the cloth (known as cross-hatching). If there is a distinct pattern why not stitch round the pattern? Does your machine have fancy stitches? How about embellishing the flap with decorative designs or with a little free machine embroidery?

When the quilting is completed, stitch round the outside with a wide zig-zag or long stitch to secure the edge to the wadding (Fig. 99)

6. Place both 'body' B pieces R/S together; sew round the curved edge using ¼"/.5cm seam allowance. Clip curve carefully (Fig. 100). Turn right side out and press. Stabilise the unsewn edges with a long stitch, keep stitching within the seam allowance.
Clip well along straight edge (Fig. 101).

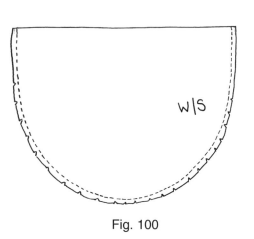

W\S

Fig. 100

Watch this space!
For all of you who think that you
know how this bag is constructed
READ THE INSTRUCTIONS
or you could GO WRONG HERE

7. Stitch a channel to hold the elastic. The channel goes round the edge of the arc side. Sew first line ¼"/½cm from edge, then sew the second line just over ½"/1cm from the first. Do measure this or the elastic will not thread through the channel (Fig. 101).

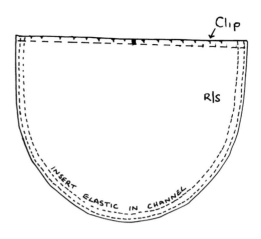

Fig. 101

8. Unpick the few stitches at the ends of the channel and slot in the elastic; use a safety pin to thread it through. Anchor the elastic 2"/5cm from one end, draw up the elastic until it measures 7"/18cm, stitch to secure 2"/5cm from the other end. This makes a gathered section 11"/28cm in length (Fig. 102).

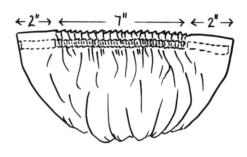

Fig. 102

9. Fold pocket section C in half and stitch along the curve to hold the layers together. Position on to the flap lining A matching-up marks and restitch to secure (Fig. 103).

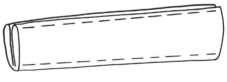

Fig. 104

10. Make the tab. With the right side on the outside, fold sides to middle then fold in half. Sew on the edge of both long sides to make a firm tab (Fig. 104). You could always use some cord or even plaited ribbon to make the tab. Stitch the tab to the quilted flap section at the correct end as in Fig. 105.

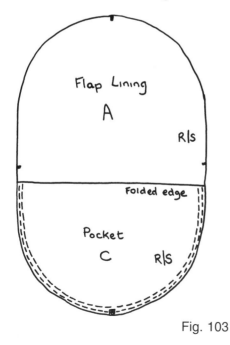

Fig. 103

11. Attach the body section to the quilted flap. Line up the marks; pin well; sew ⅜"/1cm seam allowance (see Fig. 105).

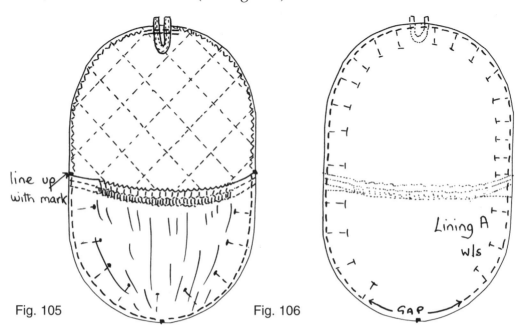

line up
with mark

Fig. 105

Lining A
w/s

GAP

Fig. 106

12. With R/S together pin the lining flap A to the quilted section A, positioning the pocket at the opposite end from the tab. The pocket will be approx 1"/2.5cm below the edge of the gathered 'body' B section. Stitch round using ⅜"/1cm seam. Use a large machine needle (14/90 or 16/100) as the work is quite thick. **Leave a gap** of approx 6"/15cm at the pocket end (Fig. 106). **Turn** right side out through the gap (don't panic if the pocket appears to be in the wrong place, just try turning the gathered sections to the other side). Sew up the hole firmly by hand.

13. Make the strap. Press ¼"/½cm seam allowance down one long side; press other side up 1¼"/3.5cm; re-press so the ¼"/½cm folded edge overlaps by ¼"/½cm. Cut wadding strips 2"/5cm wide; lay inside the strip; fold over and pin well. **If pins are placed at right angles to the seam, the work is held flatter and steadier, with the added advantage that you can sew over the pin ends.** Sew down centre fold, stitch extra lines parallel to the centre seam, run the edge of the presser foot down the first line to ensure that the next line is parallel. This makes a firm strap.

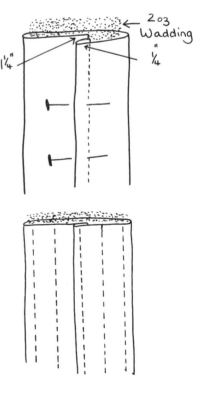

2 oz
Wadding
"
¼

1¼"

84

14. Check that the handle is the correct length, turn ends under and attach to the sides of handbag as in Fig. 107.

15. Press carefully around the flap of the bag and top-stitch to keep the lining in place (see Fig. 107). Sew carefully round on the topside (outside) using the edge of the presser foot as a guide. (Keep the inner edge of the machine foot on the side of the flap, (move the needle over or leave in the centre of the presser foot), and sew approximately ¼"(.5cm) away from the outside edge. Mark position of toggle or button and attach.

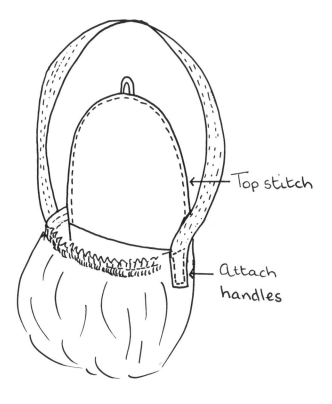

Fig. 107

WELL DONE

You have just completed your first Scrip bag, now try another. How about a textured flap using woven strips ?

Woven Textured Scrip

In addition to the previous requirements: you need -

20"/½ metre fabric (min 44"/112cm wide).
20"/½ metre iron-on lightweight vilene.

Use a generous ¼"(.75cm) seam allowance, and be consistent!

Making Up

1. Press the iron-on vilene to the back of the extra material. Cut strips 2¼"/6cm across the cloth (selvedge to selvedge); 6 to 7 strips will be required.

2. Press ⅝"/1.5cm down both the long sides, pressing towards the wrong sides; this will ensure that the edges overlap by ¼"/.5cm. Stitch down the centre back; try a decorative stitch or use the zig-zag (Fig. 108).

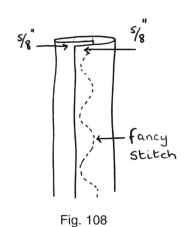

Fig. 108

3. Draw round template A on to the outer material and cut out leaving at least a 1"/2.5cm round the drawn line.

4. Lay the outer section A on a piece of 2oz wadding, ironing and pinning as described in stage 4 on page 82. *Cover* the drawn pattern with strips, cutting lengths as required. *Then* weave in and out. Pin carefully ensuring that the strips are parallel with no gaps in between. Try to keep the strips ½"(1cm) away from the sides and both ends.

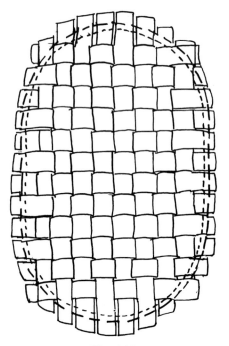

5. Place the template A on to woven design aligning with the original piece; draw round carefully. Stitch inside this pencil line to secure all the woven strips before cutting out on the drawn line (Fig. 109).

Fig. 109

Complete the construction as in the last section

Further Ideas for a Textured Scrip

Tucked-up Centre

Measure the required width of the panel. Cut a strip of material the specified width **plus the seam allowance on both sides**. Mark out the spacings and construct the tucks. You can work out the necessary length mathematically, but this is not always successful as a tiny error in the seam allowance becomes a greater error when repeated lots of times. Don't fuss: keep making tucks and when you estimate that the length is correct, give it a good press. If too long - cut off, and too short - make a few more! (To make the actual tucks see **'Tucks Textures & Pleats'** or refer to page 74.)

1. Cut out flap A in light-weight sew-in vilene. Using a pencil, lightly rule some parallel lines on the vilene to help with positioning the pieces in straight lines; cut a piece of 2oz wadding slightly larger than the vilene. Lay the vilene on the wadding; pin layers together.

2. Position tucked section down the centre checking that it is parallel to the ruled lines; pin well to secure, taking special care that the tucks are all straight. Using a long stitch setting, sew down the edge of the tucked band keeping the stitch inside the seam allowance (Fig. 110).

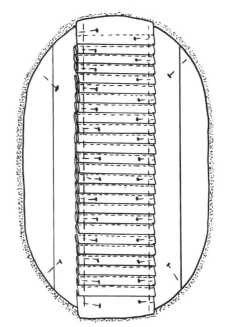

Fig. 110

3. Cut two more strips of material (does it have to be the same colour as the tucked panel?). Place R/S down on the centre section; stitch the seam, fold back and pin well. Decorate this plain area with some form of stitchery or leave blank (Fig. 111).

4. Replace the pattern template A on the completed piece aligning with the vilene, draw round and stitch just inside the drawn line. Trim back to drawn line and make up as before.

Fig. 111

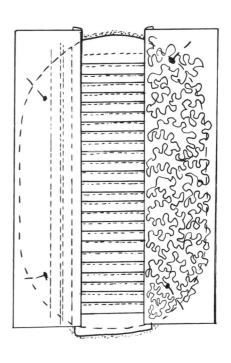

Bias `Bobble' Panel

1. Cut two pieces of material on the bias, 3"(8cm) wide x 15"(38cm) long. *Take care with directional designs - the bias pieces must be cut as mirror images.* Press 1"(2.5cm) under to the W/S on one edge. Cut out flap A in vilene, rule lines as before and place on to 2oz wadding. Cut an additional piece of material (straight grain) the length of the flap x 4"(10cm) wide. *What about a contrast colour which will be revealed as the Bias Tucks are rolled back?*

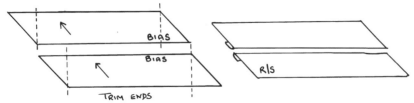

2. Lay this strip on the vilene in the centre. Position the bias strips with the pressed, (folded) sides butting up. Pin all edges, stitch both sections using ½"(1.25cm) seam through all the layers (Fig. 112).

3. Open the folds to reveal the under material, and if desired stitch down the channel with a decorative stitch (Fig. 113), either by hand or machine (this will be displayed when the tucks are rolled back). Close the tucks. Replace the template A aligning with the vilene, draw round; stitch inside the drawn line, then trim to the line.

Fig. 113

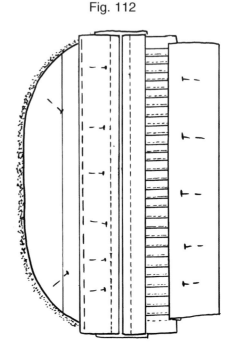

Fig. 112

4. Stay-stitch (baste) down the outer edges of the bias strips. Cut two more pieces of material and as on the previous page (stages 3 & 4) continue with the construction. Why not insert a tucked panel, then complete with a plain untextured section? *Tip: Make tucked panel twice the width required and cut in half. Then any error in the stitching or spacing will occur on both sides and could look intentional!*

5. Keeping bias tucks closed (butting up to each other and hiding the centre channel); measure in ½"(1.25cm) from the top and the bottom of flap pattern. Divide the remainder in equal amounts; mark spacings lightly with pencil or a pin. Catch the tucks down on the marks with a few small stitches. Roll back the folds to reveal the centre channel and stitch the edges of the folds down by hand or try the machine (Fig. 114). The blind hem stitch is ideal for this – see page 75. Complete as before.

There you are - four ways to make the Scrip from plain to fancy. Now make a small one or double the pattern sizes and make a huge pantechnicon of a bag to keep all the junk us females deem necessary to cart around. I wonder why it is always so essential to carry old receipts, sweetie wrappers, odd lipsticks and further related garbage all the time!

Fig. 114

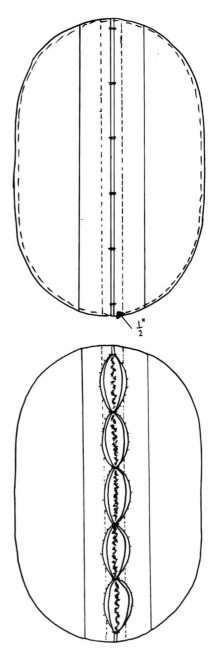

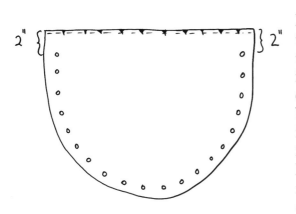

For a little extra fancy touch change the elastic for a draw-string with tassels. Instead of stitching an arc to insert the elastic simply make eyelets either with the correct tool or by hand/machine. One eyelet every inch (2.5cm) is ideal. Leave the first 2"(5cm) free at both ends where the handles will be attached. It only means making about twenty-eight of them!

More Bags

The Woven Handbag

"A handbag" said Lady Somebody-or-other in Oscar Wilde's 'Importance of being Earnest'. What about an oblong or square handbag to contain all the aforesaid collection of clutter? Featured on the cover of **'Tucks Textures & Pleats'** is a woven one. It is really easy to make, being only a boxed cushion with a handle (there is no cushion pad inside thus allowing plenty of space for stuff)!

You need: 1¼yard/1metre material, ½yard/metre 2oz wadding/batting, 10"/25cm zip fastener. *Seam allowances are ½"(1cm) throughout except for the construction of the padded bands.*

Method

1. Cut at least 7/9 strips 2½"(7cm) wide and full width of fabric. Press all the strips ¾"(2cm) in from both long sides so that the raw edges overlap by ¼"(.5cm). The bands now measure in width 1"(3cm); cut strips of 2oz wadding the length and breadth of these pressed bands. Open the seams and lay the wadding inside. Wrap up again; pin the layers together (pins at right angles to the bands); stitch down the centre of the strip securing all the layers. (Identical method to the 'Woven Effect' described in **'Tucks Textures & Pleats'**.)

2. Cut two rectangles in material 11"(28cm) x 13"(33cm); this is for the base of the weaving and it is preferable to use the same fabric as the padded strips.

3. Cut 10 x 11"(28cm) and 12 x 13"(33cm) pieces from the padded bands. Arrange the 11"(28cm) strips, butting up to each other, along the longer side of one rectangle; start and finish ½"(1.25cm) from both sides. **Pin in place**. Arrange the 13"(33cm) strips down the other side in the same way; pin in place. Weave the fabric strips in the usual over/under manner (Fig. 115). Repeat with the other rectangle of fabric.

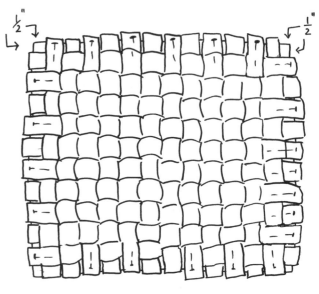

Fig. 115

Experiment with other ways of weaving to create a different effect. Why not try weaving over two strips and under one? Once the weaving is completed, pin the remaining sides. Finally stitch round the outer edge using ⅜"(1cm) seam.

4. The sides (boxing) are constructed by cutting one strip 13"(33cm) x 4"(10cm) and two strips 11"(28cm) x 4"(10cm), plus one strip 13"(33cm) x 5½"(14cm) - extra width to allow for zip insertion. Insert zip into this last strip and *leave it open a fraction.* (For a quick and easy method of zip insertion see the Finishing Chapter in **'Tucks Textures and Pleats'**.) Once the zip has been inserted the strip should measure 4"(10cm) wide - if more trim back to 4"(10cm) if less than 4"(10cm) trim the other strips to match.

All the strips must measure the same width.

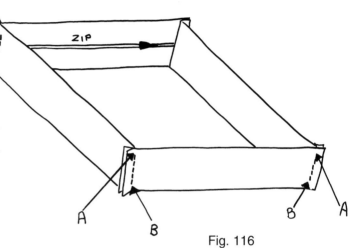

5. Make the boxing by stitching the strips together end to end with ⅜"(1cm) seam allowance (Fig. 116); *leave ⅜"(1cm) unstitched at both ends of seam A/B.*

Fig. 116

6. Attach to one side of the woven panel as in Fig. 117. Using same S/A stitch from A to A pushing the seams out of the way; *start and finish each side individually.*

At no point must the seams of the boxing be caught in the corners.

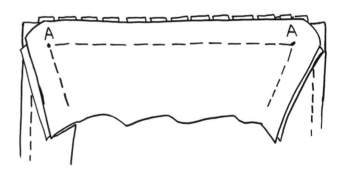

Fig. 117

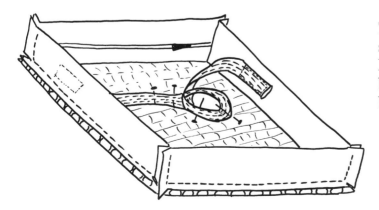

7. Make a handle as in stage 13 page 84. Attach handle to both sides of the boxing; pin well to the base.

8. Attach the other side as before. Turn the bag R/S out. Now curse, as you did not **remember to leave the zip open** and you will have to feel the end through all the layers!

To line the bag, simply construct a further bag without a zip and obviously no weaving; turn W/S out and drop into the outer casing; slip stitch the lining to the zip. *Be careful not to stitch too close to the zip or it will not open.*

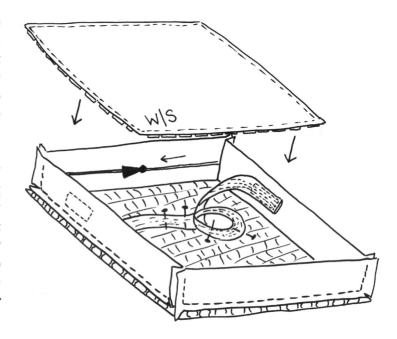

That is it - one boxed 'cushion' handbag. Now you can make any size of bags and/or a boxed cushion

A Sausage or Bolster Bag

The basic design of a sausage bag is a cylinder with a zip and handles or handle. The cylinder part of the bag can be a plain piece of material or could be textured.

Sadly there are mathematics to be done. One of those Grecian bods, Pythagoras (or is it Archimedes?) creeps into the problem. One of these had his toe stuck down the plughole, the other fiddled around with circles and triangles. I shall plump for the former - Pythagoras. He did nasty things with areas and circumferences of circles, and worked out a formula which for some unknown reason had culinary overtones being all to do with pies; so you need to know how to calculate a Grecian pie. Very simply, multiply 3.14 ounces of fat by twice the amount of flour and, **Hey presto!** you will get the length of the pastry round the edge. Very elementary Dr. Watson! The snag is how much flour do you use?

Now, to be serious, decide on the diameter (width from side to side) of the circular ends of the bag, divide this measurement by 2 to get the radius (width from centre to outer edge); multiply this measurement by 2 x 3.14 to give the total circumference.

10"(25cm) diameter ÷ 2 = 5"(12.5) radius
5"(12.5) radius x 2 x 3.14 = 31.4"(78.5cm) circumference

(The more astute of you will realise that you only need to know the diameter then simply multiply it by 3.14; there is no need to divide by 2 then multiply by 2, but you have to know the radius at some point to set the compass. Magically this works in both inches or centimetres or whatever form of units you choose to measure in.)

Having worked out the circumference you know the length of fabric required to fit round that particular circle; *now add ½"(1cm) seam allowance to both ends. The total length now measures 32.4"(82.5cm) i.e. 31.4"(78.5cm) + 2 x ½"(.5cm) if using the 10"(25cm) diameter circle.*

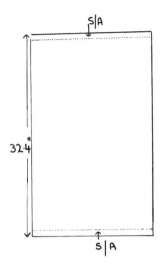

1. Draw the selected circle on paper with a compass. Remember to set the compass for the *radius* (½ diameter). Mark where the compass point was inserted; *add the seam allowance by extending the compass measurement ½"(1cm)*; re-draw the circle and cut out. You have now made the template for the ends *including the seam allowance.*

2. Make up the end sections using whatever design you choose. All the outer sections of the bag should be quilted on to wadding, either 2oz or even 4oz. Don't forget to stitch round the outside of the circle to secure the fabric to the wadding.

3. Now construct the main (body) part of the bag, *remembering to add the seam allowances to both the length and the width.* Thus if the desired width is 20"(50cm), the ends as before - 10"(25cm) diameter - you need a rectangle 21"(52cm) x 32.4"(82.5cm) in total. *The section with the zip inserted has to be included in this section.*

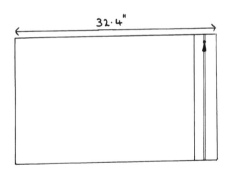

4. The simplest method of inserting the zip is to put it into a strip then attach the strip to the main piece; check the measurement and trim the main body so the final length is correct.

5. Add the handles at this stage. Make up the required length either one long one or two short ones; stitch to the bag spacing evenly on the 'body' section. Dividing the 'body' in three will give a fair guide to the positioning. (You may prefer to position the handles differently to suit the design of the bag or for the best optical appearance.)

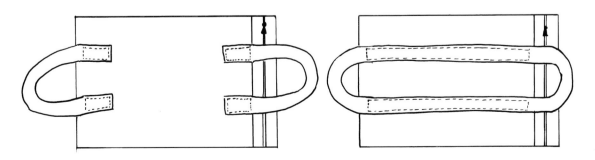

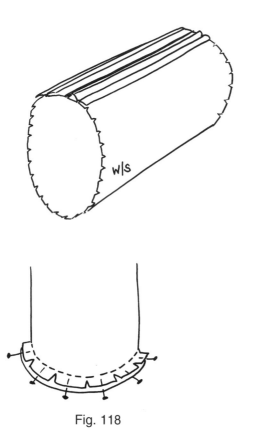

6. Join both ends of the 'body' section across the width using the correct seam allowance. Clip the circumference (outer edges of 'body'); pin well to the ends and stitch round (Fig. 118); *watch the seam allowance* (it will only fit on the original circle edge). Should it not quite fit, there is nothing like a bit of push and shove with the odd prayer or two, and I bet it will go in. Turn R/S out.

Fig. 118

7. To line it, cut identically sized pieces and make another bag but without any wadding; leave a gap the same length and in the same place as the zip. Turn W/S out and drop into the outer casing; attach the lining to the zip and catch to the ends in several places.

There you are - one Sausage Bag!

Hats Ahoy!

It was very difficult to resist the temptation to call this section a 'Tucked-up Titfer' or a 'Textured Topper', but not everyone appreciates my eccentric sense of humour. In fact this particular hat has caused much merriment in the past.

I had the pleasure of going to the Quilt Festival in Houston to teach and generally promote 'nipping and tucking'. For general assistance and as a companion, I took my son with me. We had a splendid time participating in all the events, especially a lunchtime fashion show designed to promote the various products on display at the Festival. To cut an exceedingly long story short I had decided to take part in this affair: my son Alexander would describe the virtues of the garments over the p.a. and I would prance down the catwalk. When the day dawned he was unwell and in no condition to speak; so we had to have a role reversal. He pranced wearing the Jacket - too short in the arms by yards, the Belt - only just went round him, the Hat - looking like a pimple and carrying the Handbag! Alexander is much taller and generally considerably larger than I am.

So this long lanky lad leapt on to the catwalk swinging the bag round and round like a pin-wheel, clutching the product - **'Tucks Textures & Pleats'** to his chest. He stood there gesticulating wildly to the various bits that I was describing in my most effusive manner. Then he dropped the book, bent over revealing his manly posterior to one half of the room while the other half watched as his hat fell off. The belt slipped to the ground and horrors of horrors I realised that he was still wearing those scruffy trainers with the laces all undone. My dream of taking the American fashion scene by storm was shattered. What had happened to the svelte mannequin graciously swaying down the runway elegantly modelling these couture garments, while the audience sat in stunned amazement at the ingenuity and talent paraded before them? Instead everybody roared with laughter and wouldn't stop! To my incredulity when I was signing books later in the day, lots of people didn't want my signature but that of 'Super-model' Alex! Hmm, how are the mighty fallen!

Here is how to make the Hat

I am no milliner, but this method seemed to produce a pretty good hat. There are many other ways of creating an interesting 'titfer', of which you will probably be aware. But for the 'Chapeau à la Rayment' read on.

You need: 15"(38cm) square + extra ¼ yd/mtr of pelmet Vilene or similar stiffener
Approximately ¾ yd/mtr medium-weight calico, toning threads
All seam allowances are ½"(1cm) unless stated otherwise

Method

1. Find an old sun-hat or bonnet that will give you the correct size and shape of your head. By some means fair or foul draw round the inner rim. I do this by placing a large sheet of paper across the underside of the hat; pin in place then with a sharp pencil dot round the opening. Remove from the hat and join the dots; neaten the line all round to make reasonably even. Add ¼"(.5cm) to the outside of this line (central hole must be a little larger to allow for the bulk of the seams when linking the crown to the brim). The brim will be measured from this new line.

Very carefully make the brim by making more dots 3"(8cm) from the outer central line; join the dots. This width can be changed if desired. Cut on both lines forming the template for the brim (Fig. 119).

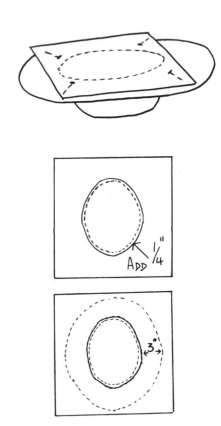

Fig. 119

2. Draw round template on to the pelmet vilene; cut carefully on this line - the centre section will be the stiffening for the crown. Place vilene shape on the calico, pin, *cut two out adding ½"(1cm) to the inner circle edge only.* Sandwich the pelmet vilene between both pieces of calico, matching the outer edges. Pin well with pins radiating out from the centre (Fig. 120).

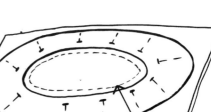

Fig. 120

3. Tack/baste layers together keeping close to the outer edge. Tack/baste ¾ (2cm) inside the inner edge; ensure the tacking/basting remains on and close to the edge of the vilene (Fig. 121).

4. Working from the centre out, following the inner line of tacking/basting, sew rows of stitches. Use the edge of the presser foot as a guide. Continue until the outer edge is reached (Fig. 122). Sew closely round the outer edge with a short stitch length to secure the layers.

5. Seal the raw outer edges with satin stitch. (See page 78 for stitching technique.) Remove any tacking stitching that shows.

6. From the remaining fabric cut two strips of calico and one strip of pelmet vilene for the sides of the crown. Decide on the height of the sides of the crown. (Hat in photograph had 3"(8cm) sides.) This can be of any size: it purely depends on personal preference and the size of your 'bonce' (head). Measure round the *inner hole of the template*; using this measurement cut the vilene and the calico *adding ½"(1cm) seam allowance to both sides and ends of strips of the calico only*

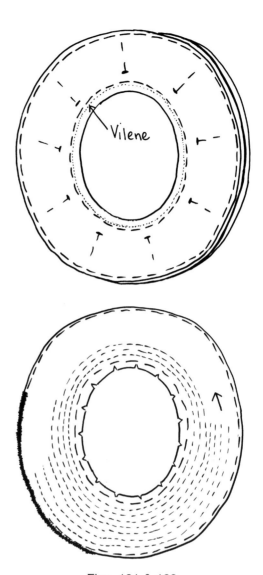

Figs. 121 & 122

7. Using the centre rounded section of the pelmet vilene as a template, place on the calico; pin and cut two pieces (*adding ½"(1cm) seam allowance as before*).

8. Join the ends of one side section using ½"(1cm) seam. Clip both edges; attach to one of the crown sections (Fig. 123) with a ½"(1cm) seam. Repeat with the remaining strip and crown section for the lining. Turn one of these R/S out.

Fig. 123

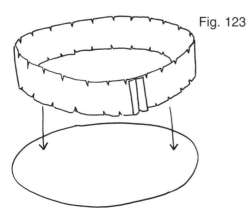

Remember it will only fit correctly on the original circle edge: i.e. before the seam allowances were added.

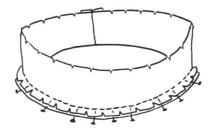

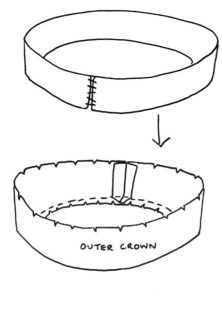

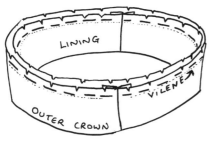

OUTER CROWN

LINING

VILENE

OUTER CROWN

Fig 124

9. Link the ends of the vilene together with a faggoting or zig-zag tack/baste stitch. Place in the 'R/S out' crown; pin and tack/baste to the sides. (The vilene will be ½"(1cm) shorter than the width of the crown sides.) Lay the crown circle of pelmet vilene in the top; pin; tack/baste to the seams (Fig. 124). Similar to lining a cake tin!

10. Insert the lining. Tack/baste ½"(1cm) round lower edge. This tacking will be just beside the vilene edge. Position the seam opposite to the one on the outer section.

11. Clip the inner edge of brim before joining to the crown *by hand* (not possible to do on the machine!) using ½"(1cm) seam and small firm stitches (Fig. 125). Trim the seams well. Try on! Should your head have expanded with excitement, unpick and stitch a larger seam.

12. Cover these raw edges inside the brim with some binding. Cut 1½"(4cm) bias strip x circumference of inner brim. Attach to the inside of the crown (R/S's together); bring the binding over the raw edges and slip stitch to the lining (Fig. 126). It is possible to cheat by machining the binding to the brim before linking the two pieces; although speedier it can cause problems. Think it out carefully before you do this or the binding may end up caught in the seams, facing the wrong way or cause distortion in some form. The hat can now be embellished as desired. Try a draped scarf or tie on some dyed silk or chiffon. I choose to make a 'Bias Bobble' band to decorate the crown.

Fig. 125   Fig. 126

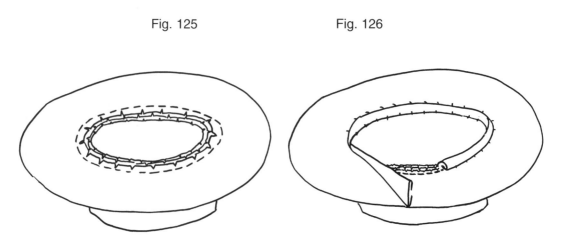

'Bias Bobble Band'

Method

1. Measure the circumference of the crown. Cut *two x 2"(2.5cm) wide bias strips* this length *adding ½"(1cm)seam allowance to either end*. In addition cut *one x 1½"(4cm) wide straight grain strip* the same length as the bias strips. Find centre of this strip by folding in half lengthways and gently ironing; lay flat when finished. Press one edge of both bias strips under by ¾"(2cm). Place on the *1½"(4cm)* strip, butting the pressed edges to the centre crease (Fig. 127). Pin well through all the layers.

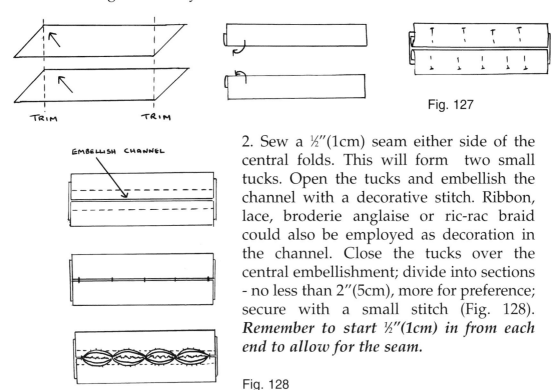

Fig. 127

2. Sew a ½"(1cm) seam either side of the central folds. This will form two small tucks. Open the tucks and embellish the channel with a decorative stitch. Ribbon, lace, broderie anglaise or ric-rac braid could also be employed as decoration in the channel. Close the tucks over the central embellishment; divide into sections - no less than 2"(5cm), more for preference; secure with a small stitch (Fig. 128). *Remember to start ½"(1cm) in from each end to allow for the seam.*

Fig. 128

3. Roll back the tucks to reveal the decoration; sew the edges of the tucks down by hand or machine. Yet again the blind hem stitch is useful (see page 75 for instructions).

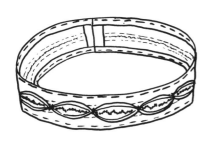

Fig. 129

4. With R/S's facing join the ends to form a circle; gently press the seams open and flat. Turn the band over and on the W/S press the long edges in by ¼"(.5cm) towards the back. Turn back to the R/S and very carefully sew as close to the edges as possible (Fig. 129). This will neaten the edge, ready for applying to the crown.

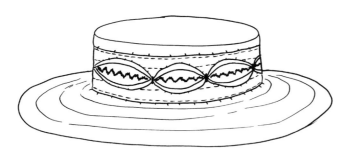

5. Slip the band on to the crown; stitch round both edges with a small hand stitch. Use of a curved needle may be advantageous.

(For more information on the 'Bias Bobble' see **'Tucks Textures & Pleats'** pages 40 - 46.)

Now the crowning touch.

How about a cluster of petals or a posy of flowers? Make up some three-dimensional flowers *as described in the 'Textured Landscapes' chapter.

Imagine the scene.

She drifted down the catwalk, her exquisite haute-couture gown rustling as she moved. Carelessly tossed over one seductive shoulder swung a superb silken bolero fabulously pleated in an array of colours. Pertly balanced on her cloud of auburn hair was a stunning creation of creamy satin encrusted with delicate roses. Small pearls nestled like dewdrops amongst the softly curling petals. The audience was enchanted!

*'Course you could always go to 'Woolies' and buy some fake plastic ones, but would it be the same?

Tucked-up

Fabric Baskets

A little bit of textural nonsense for you. Having ploughed your way through reams of arduous mathematics and struggled with grains, sizes and complicated folding etc., take a moment of light relief and tuck-up a basket or two.

This is ideal for Christmas and could be a centre-piece on the table filled with little novelties, or pop some goodies into it and give it to a friend. It's one of those silly gifts eminently suitable for any age from small children to the much more mature – certainly one up on yet another box of 'smellies'.

I think that we all have drawers of odd talcum powders and curious bath lotions that you can't give away again unless you can remember positively who gave it to you in first place. I am sure that some people are organised enough to pop a note in with the gift 'Do not give to ....'. There have been times when forgetting to purchase that small something for a friend's birthday or when looking for a small gift to take to a supper party as a thank you for the hostess, I have rooted through my drawer then been struck by the horrid thought – did she give this to me in the first place? Imagine the embarrassment when you realise that she did. There will be a slightly agonised expression on the hostess' face as she voices her thanks in that somewhat insincere sweet way. So do not fall into this trap – make a new present.

Template for Round Fabric Basket

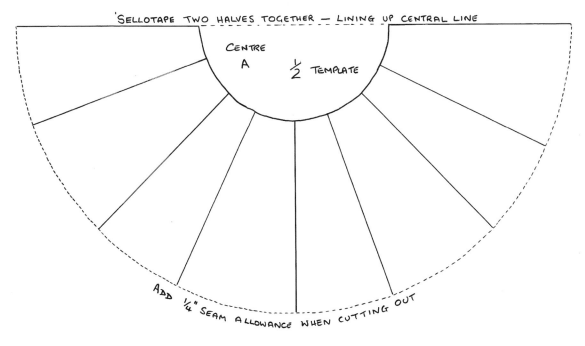

Round Fabric Basket

This basket can be made in any type of material from a lightweight furnishing or chintz to fine cottons and lawns (fine cotton fabric with a crisp coating). It looks best made from two toning materials – one for the outside and one for the lining.

You need:-

2 x 13"(34cm) squares - (one in each colour)
3 x 2½"(7cm)wide x 18"(46cm)long strips* - (two in one colour/one in the other)
1 x 1½"(4.5cm) wide x 25"(65cm)long bias strip
¼ yard/metre 4oz wadding/batting + some more scraps for stuffing

Remember to cut the strips from selvedge to selvedge across the fabric.

The Template

Half the template is shown on the previous page drawn to 1/3rd scale. Use a photocopier and scale up by 300% to make the radius of the half-template 6"(15cm) which forms a 12"(30cm) circle when placed on a fold. Make two copies of this size and stick together to make the full template, or trace the template on to a folded sheet of tracing/grease-proof paper; open out and re-trace the other half. Failing to have photocopier facilities to hand you will have to draw your own. It is not difficult.

Take a large sheet of paper, minimum size 13"(34cm) square. Find the centre and with a compass set at 2"(5cm), draw a 4"(10cm) circle in the middle. Keeping the point in the same place, then set compass at 6"(15cm) and draw a 12"(30cm) circle.

Should the inevitable happen and the compass will not extend to this measurement, do not rush out and buy a new one. Simply draw the largest circle that you can and add the little extra by measuring with a ruler. Make a small series of dots and join by eye – well, use a pencil, it makes better marks.

Mark the centre (where the compass point was inserted) with a cross and put your protractor on the cross. Make an mark alternating every 20° and every 25° i.e. put a dot on 20°, 45°, 65°, 90°, 110°, 135°, 155°, 180°. Turn the protractor and repeat on the other half (Fig. 130).

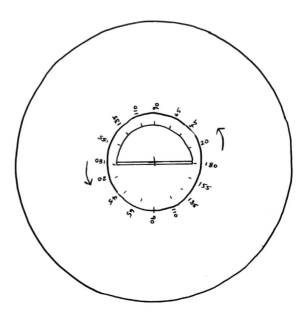

Fig. 130

Align a ruler with the central cross and one of the marks, then rule a line from the outside of the inner circle to the inside of the outer circle (Fig. 131). Repeat with all the marks.

Make a tracing of this template.

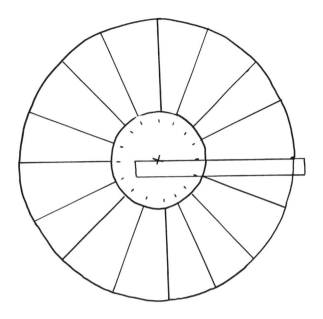

Fig. 131

Transferring Template to the Fabric

Trace the template on to one piece of fabric.

Should the chosen materials be thin or of a light colour, by re-drawing the lines on the template with a black pen, you will probably be able to trace directly on to the fabric. If this isn't possible, try taping the pattern to the window and tape the fabric over it, letting the light shine through (sunny weather is best). Naturally, when you want the light it will be dark outside, or the skies are grey, it's raining and/or it's the middle of a wintry afternoon when the sun has not been seen for days (normal English scenario)! Try a makeshift light box - bright desk lamp under a glass topped table or sheet of perspex balanced on two chairs with a desk lamp underneath.

An alternative way to transfer the template is by copying on to a large sheet of paper and pinning well to one of the pieces of material and stitching on the lines. Tear the paper away when completed. This will be destroyed when you sew. ***Do not use the master copy.***

If you are lucky enough to have a supply of 'Freezer' paper, this is preferable to plain paper. 'Freezer' paper is used in America to wrap food and can be purchased in most U.S.A. supermarkets, but it's not normally available in the U.K except from some 'Lakeland Plastics' shops. (The wrappings of the reams of photocopying paper can be used.) It has a waxed shiny side and a matt side. The template is traced on the matt side, cut out and then pressed with the *waxed* surface down on to the fabric. This adheres to the material allowing you to stitch all the lines as above then remove by tearing away. (The waxing has no apparent effect on the fabric surface.)

Making the Basket

1. Lay both pieces of fabric W/S together. Cut a piece of 4oz wadding approximately the same size as the centre circle. Insert wadding between the layers, lining up with the centre. Pin well through all the layers (Fig. 132).

2. Stitch round the centre circle; sew down every line radiating out from the centre circle to the outer one (Fig. 132). Start with a very small stitch then increase the stitch length to the normal size (saves having to tie all the ends off).

3. *Cut round the outer circle leaving ¼"(.5cm) seam allowance.* Carefully rip off the paper from all the sections including the very centre. Embellish and strengthen the centre by stitching in a spiral.

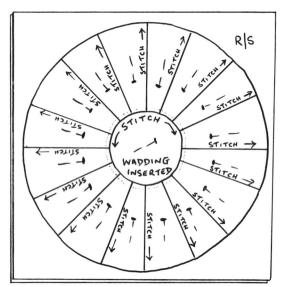

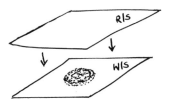

Fig. 132

Start the spiral by positioning the edge of the presser foot on the central circle line; sew round gradually drifting the presser foot inwards (sewing further from the line) until the edge of the presser foot is lined up with the circle.

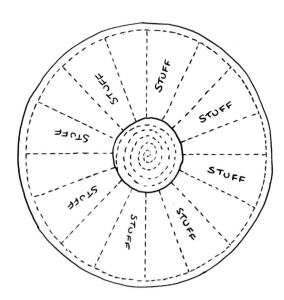

Continue sewing round and round – keeping the edge of the presser foot flush with the previous stitch line – until you reach the middle. Stop: make a few very small stitches on the spot and cut the thread ends off.

4. Stuff the larger (every other) wedge sections *only*. Tear the wadding into small pieces, and stuff the sections full but not too firmly. Stitch round the outer edge following the traced line or ¼"(.5cm) in from the outside.

5. Form pleats by matching the seams on the unpadded sections; pinch together and pin; flatten out the dart that is formed. Sew round again to anchor these pleats (Fig. 133). These darts make the basket shape -
large darts = small basket rim, small darts = large rim.

6. Make the handle by pressing ¼"(.5cm) down one long side of all three strips; press the sides to the centre overlapping the seams by ¼"(.5cm). Cut three thin pieces of wadding the length and breadth of the pressed band.

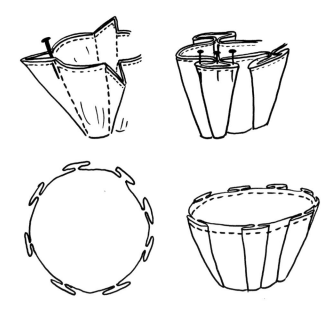

Fig. 133

Fig. 134

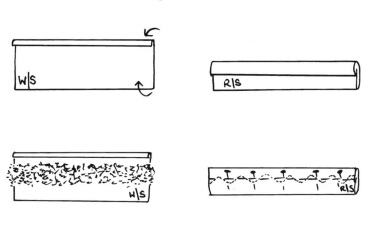

Open up the band and lay the wadding inside; fold over (wadding is now wrapped in the fabric); pin the layers together with the pins at right angles to the strip (Fig. 134).

7. Machine down the centre line using a wide zig-zag or long stitch length, stitching through all the layers (as in previous bag handles). Trim strips to the same length. Stitch all three strips together at one end; plait together (plaiting is right band over centre, left band over centre etc.). Continue plaiting for 12/13½"(30/34cm); stitch ends to secure the plait (Fig. 135).

8. Attach plaited handle to the outside of the basket; line up with the outer edge and stitch firmly back and forth following the original sewing (Fig. 136). Trim off any excess.

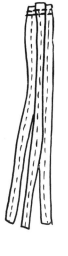

Fig. 135

9. Complete the basket by binding the raw edge. Cut ends of binding straight. Match up raw edge with basket rim; fold ¼"(.5cm) over at the start (Fig. 137); stitch in place with a fractionally bigger seam allowance than before (should conceal all previous rows of stitching).

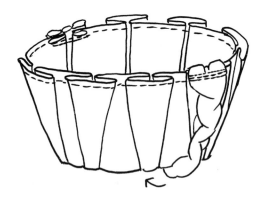 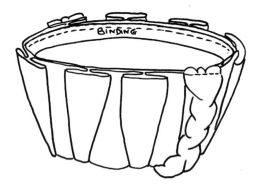

Fig.136

10. Fold binding up and over the raw edge; turn under approximately ¼"(.5cm); slip/hem stitch in place. Fold handle up and over the binding and stitch well to secure.

Fig. 137

More Baskets

Exactly the same construction techniques can be used to make any size of basket with more or less padded sections.

Change the measurements of the original circles to increase or decrease the size; remember to modify the length of handle strips and the bias band.

Change the proportions of the wedges by altering the degrees (the total of degrees used must add up to 360°).

Change the basic shape of the basket - try an oval. Ovoid baskets are excellent for holding Easter Eggs! Draw the initial design using oval shapes as opposed to round; mark the centre as before and use the same method for ascertaining the degree divisions.

Having experimented with all these ideas myself it occurred to me that a square basket could be made on the same principle; so here is a:-

Square Basket

1. Cut two 12½"(31cm) squares of fabric. Rule parallel lines as shown in Fig. 138 on one of the pieces, preferably the inner piece, - then the pencil lines will not show. *Set the lines in by ¼"(.5cm) on all sides* (measurements are shown in inches only but can be converted to metric if required).

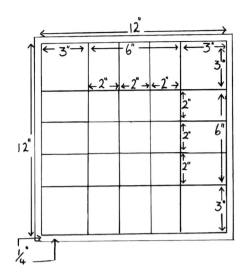

Fig. 138

2. Cut 6"(15cm) square of 4oz wadding and insert in the centre between the layers. Sew all the ruled lines.

Sew carefully across the central section because the extra thickness of the wadding may cause the layers to creep and you will get a dragged appearance in the materials. Use of a 'walking foot' or slackening off the pressure on the presser foot may solve the problem.

3. Pad all twelve oblong pockets with torn up wadding. Match up the side seams and pin together. Using the zipper foot carefully sew the seams (Fig. 139).

Panic - there is a basket with strange corners!

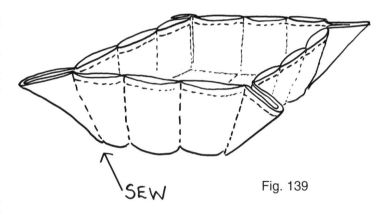

SEW

Fig. 139

4. Flatten darts, pinning carefully to the top edge of the basket. Stitch round this edge to anchor darts and close pockets. Trim or tuck in excess (Fig. 140).

5. Cut out strips for handles and strips for binding (page 102). Make up handle and attach as in stages 6 - 8 (page 105). Complete the basket with the binding as in stage 9 (page 106)

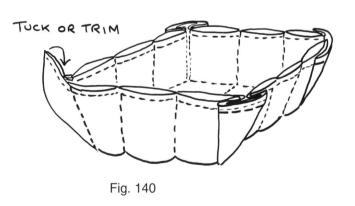

TUCK OR TRIM

Fig. 140

There you are - baskets for everyone!

Conclusion

Once you reach this page, there will probably be a large pile of U.F.O.'s (unfinished objects), but I trust that you will have had some fun playing with the methods and experimenting with all the techniques. Although we all have such good intentions, many of the pieces will never get completed. The trouble is that there is never enough time in the day to do all that we want; little things like work get in the way.

When I start getting engrossed in any project, all my friends and family get somewhat ignored, which is really most unfair. I try very hard to keep the balance between recreation and work but when an idea starts to flow - hang the housework, give the cat another goldfish and play. This explains why the house is dusty, the garden overrun, the ironing basket filled to overflowing, there's no more washing-up liquid and only three goldfish left in the bowl. **NOT** the best way to conduct a well-ordered life, but tomorrow I can clean, mow, iron and shop. (Hopefully it will be raining so I won't be able to cut the grass, the dust will not show so much, I will get wet if I walk to the shops and the ironing can always wait; in which case I shall just have to play a bit more.)

There were several ideas that I wanted to put into this book, but ran out of time: so there will be yet another tome in a year or so. The next volume will contain a few more textural designs plus some really easy ways to cheat at Patchwork and Quilting, as well as various projects to make. By the time this is published, I should have achieved my latest ambition. No one believes that all I want to do is retire to a small cottage in the country, plant my garden, make new quilts for the bed, gather fruit for jam and wine making and purchase a Great Dane. My intention is to sally forth and teach at selected places, then dive home and be domestic for a while, walk the dog, write a page or two, put my feet up and/or veg out down the pub. (One day I might even complete the crossword in the newspaper.)

The best laid plans of mice and women do not always come to fruition, and rather than end up peacefully in the cottage, I shall probably be found gibbering about 'Nipping and Tucking' in some far flung corner of the globe surrounded by a heap of calico samples.

Have a good day!

(N.B. In case you wondered why there were not so many multiples of exclamation marks as in the last publication; here are just a few to make up!!!!!!!!!!!!!)

Glossary

Backing: The fabric used underneath a sample or the underside of a cushion or quilt.

Baste: Securing of layers with a long stitch to prevent movement.

Batting: Wadding or filling frequently made from polyester fibres used in between or underneath fabric for quilting purposes.

Bias: Diagonal of the woven grain (45 degrees to the selvedge).

Borders: Fabric attached to the outer edges to frame the sample.

Broderie Anglais: Openwork embroidery frequently made in pure cotton fabric.

Calico: Plain woven strong cotton cloth (sometimes bleached) with a distinctive fleck in the weave. (**British definition**.) Called **Muslin** in the U.S.A.

Catch: Several small stitches in the same place for securing an edge/corner of material.

Cathedral Window Patchwork: Traditional design constructed from folded and stitched squares.

Chintz: Close-weave shiny cotton cloth with a resin coating for that characteristic sheen.

Colour Wheel: All the colours of the spectrum (red, orange, yellow, green, blue, indigo, violet) arranged as segments of a circle.

Crettonne: A washable hard-wearing fabric similar to unglazed chintz; liable to shrink.

Gabardine: A lightweight closely woven fabric with a prominent diagonal rib.

Grain: Direction of the weave. Weft fibres run across from selvedge to selvedge. Warp fibres are parallel to the selvedge.

Log Cabin Patchwork: Traditional designs made from strips of material frequently found in a square format. The square is often divided diagonally into light and dark colours.

Mercerised Cotton: Polished and treated to look like silk.

Muslin: Fine soft cotton fabric resembling gauze in appearance. (**British definition**.)

Pelmet Vilene: Thick, stiff interfacing made from bonded fibres.

Pineapple Log Cabin Patchwork: More complicated version of Log Cabin design which on completion has a resemblance to pineapples.

Pin Tucks: Fine tucks sometimes enclosing a cord.

Pin-wheel: Rotation of one shape at 90° round a central point.

R/S:; Right side of material.

Ruche/Ruching: Gathered material often in a strip, used for decorative effect.

Satin Stitch: The zig-zag effect produced by increasing the stitch width and decreasing the stitch length on the sewing machine.

Seam Allowance: Distance between the stitch line and the edge of the fabric.

Seminole: Traditional strip patchwork from the Seminole Indians of America.

Selvedge/selvage: The firm edges of the fabric running parallel to the warp threads.

Somerset/Folded Patchwork: Design made with folded squares of fabric, worked from the centre outwards on lines relating to equal points of the compass

Space Dyed Threads: Fibres dyed in a variety of separate colours.

Stay stitching: Securing of layers with a long stitch to prevent movement.

Tack: Securing of layers with a long stitch to prevent movement.

Vilene: Interfacing developed from bonded fibres

W/S: Wrong or underside of fabric.

Wadding: Batting or filling frequently made from polyester fibres used in between or underneath fabric for quilting purposes.

Index

List of Shops & Suppliers

*Locations of Workshops taught by Jennie Rayment

Austin Sykes
74/77 St. Pancras
Chichester, West Susses
Tel: 01243 782139

*The Bramble Patch
West Street
Weedon
Northants NN7 4QU
Tel: 01327 342212

*The Cotton Patch
1285 Stratford Road
Hall Green
Birmingham B28 9AJ
Tel: 0121 702 2840
Fax: 0121 778 5924

*Country Crafts
10a St. Mary's Walk
Hailsham, East Sussex
Tel: 01323 442271

*Country Threads
2 Pierrepoint Place
Bath BA1 1JX
Tel: 01225 480056

*Creative Quilting
3 Bridge Road
Hampton Court
Surrey KT8 9EU
Tel: 0181 941 7075

*Embsay Mills
Embsay
Skipton, North Yorks
Tel: 01756 700946

Fourshire Books
17 High Street
Moreton-in-the-Marsh
Gloucs GL56 0AF
01608 651451

Green Hill
27 Bell Street
Romsey
Hampshire SO51 8GY
Tel: 01794 517973

*Missenden Abbey
(Teaching only)
Great Missenden
Bucks HP16 0BD
Tel: 01494 890297

Moor Silks & Yarns
Paddons Row
Brook Street
Tavistock
Devon PL19 0HF
Tel: 01822 612624

*Needle & Thread
80 High Street
Horsell, Woking
Surrey GU21 4SZ

*Needlepatch
Mangerton Mill
Mangerton, Bridport
Dorset DT6 3SG
Tel: 01308 485689

Patchworkers Paradise
16 East Street
Blandford Forum
Dorset DTII 7DR
Tel: 01258 456099

Patchwork Plus
129 Station Road
Cark-in-Cartmel
Grange-over-Sands
Cumbria LA11 7NY
Tel: 01539 559009

Pick 'n Choose
(Calico supplier)
56 Station Road
Northwich
Cheshire CW9 5RB
Tel: 01606 415523
Fax: 01606 47255

*Purely Patchwork
23 High Street
Linlithgow
Scotland EH49 7AB
Tel/Fax: 01506 846200

Quilters Cottage
60 Bridge Street
Garstang, Preston
Lancs PR3 1YB
Tel: 01995 603929

*Quilt Basics
Unit 19, Chiltern House
Waterside, Chesham
Bucks HP5 1PS
Tel: 01494 791401
Fax: 01494785202

*Quilters Haven
68 High Street
Wickham Market
Suffolk IP13 0QU
Tel: 01728 746275

*The Quilt Room
20 West Street
Dorking
Surrey RH4 1BL
Tel: 01306 740739
Fax: 01306 877407

*Red Cottage Crafts
1 Rawdon Court
Main Street, Moira
Co. Armagh BT67 0LQ
Tel: 01846 619172

*West Dean College
(Teaching only)
West Dean
Chichester
West Sussex PO18 0QZ
Tel: 01243 811301

*Village Fabrics
Unit 7a
Bushells Business Est.
Hithercroft, Wallingford
Oxon OX10 9DD
Tel: 01491 836178
Fax: 01491 825565

*You Toucan Quilt
Windsor House
Greville Road
Bedminister
Bristol BS3 1LL
Tel: 0117 9632599

International Distributors

Quilter's Resources Inc.
P.O. Box 148850, Chicago,
Illinois 60614, U.S.A.
Tel: 773 278 5695
Fax: 773 278 1348

Margaret Barrett Distributors Ltd.
19 Beasley Avenue,
P.O. Box 12-034, Penrose,
Auckland, New Zealand
Tel: 64-9-525 6142
Fax: 64-9-525 6382

'Tucks Textures & Pleats' Video

Village Fabrics in conjunction with Jennie Rayment are going to make a video on the techniques described in the previous book **'Tucks Textures & Pleats'**. This will be available towards the end of 1997 and will be available from Village Fabrics (address as above). It will be compatible with both U.K. and U.S.A. video systems.